General Editor Alastair Service

THE BUILDINGS OF BRITAIN
ANGLO-SAXON
AND NORMAN

Alastair Service is the author of *Edwardian Architecture* (1977), *The Architects of London: 1066 to the present day* (1979), *A Guide to the Megaliths of Europe* (1979, paperback 1981), *Edwardian Interiors* (1982) and other books. He is a Committee Member of the Victorian Society.

Uniform with this volume in the series *The Buildings of Britain*:

General Editor Alastair Service

THE BUILDINGS OF BRITAIN
ANGLO-SAXON
AND NORMAN

A Guide and Gazetteer
ALASTAIR SERVICE

Photographs by the author

Barrie & Jenkins

London   Melbourne   Sydney   Auckland   Johannesburg

To M.L.C.

Barrie & Jenkins Ltd
An imprint of the Hutchinson Publishing Group
17–21 Conway Street, London W1P 6JD

Hutchinson Group (Australia) Pty Ltd
30–32 Cremorne Street, Richmond South, Victoria 3121
PO Box 151, Broadway, New South Wales 2007

Hutchinson Group (NZ) Ltd
32–34 View Road, PO Box 40–086, Glenfield, Auckland 10

Hutchinson Group (SA) (Pty) Ltd
PO Box 337, Bergvlei 2012, South Africa

Designed and produced for Barrie & Jenkins Ltd by
Bellew & Higton Publishers Ltd
17–21 Conway Street, London W1P 6JD

First published 1982

© Alastair Service 1982

Photoset in Goudy Old Style by V & M Graphics Ltd, Aylesbury, Bucks
Printed and bound in Great Britain by
Penshurst Press Ltd

ISBN 0 09 150130 X (cased)
ISBN 0 09 150131 8 (paper)

CONTENTS

PREFACE

This book is designed to assist the growing number of people who enjoy the high pleasures of travelling to look at historic buildings. These travellers need to know which of the buildings are the most rewarding to visit, where they are, and how each building fits into the architectural development and social history of its time. The first chapters outline with illustrations the story of each type of building's development during the period – houses, churches, castles and other kinds – and the historical background. The second part is an extensive but selective gazeteer, each entry with descriptive notes on a building or town of particular interest, and each one marked on the accompanying maps with an appropriate symbol. Readers can therefore find out which areas of the country have many buildings of that kind worth visiting and, vice versa, can see what there is to look at in any region they may be visiting.

ACKNOWLEDGEMENTS

I have been helped by many people with this Anglo-Saxon and Norman volume. I would like to thank especially the owners of Norman houses who allowed me to visit their homes; the clergy and staff of churches who have taken time to point out many things to me; my late father, my brother-in-law John Hemming, and Sir Alfred Clapham for introducing me to the pleasures of Norman Romanesque; Sir Nikolaus Pevsner for the help he has given me both personally and through his books; Margaret Crowther for helping me to devise the series over lunch one day; Louisa Service and our children – as well as many other close friends and relatives – for their company and varying enjoyment of Romanesque buildings all over western Europe; Dr H. M. Taylor, Margaret Wood and Professor G. Zarnecki for their illuminating scholarship; Zandria Pauncefort for her assistance with background material on the Anglo-Saxon period; and Frances Kelly, Antony Wood and Gladys Horton for their expertise in preparing both book and series.

INTRODUCTION

The quest for Anglo-Saxon and Norman architecture and sculpture will take the seeker to churches in many of the prettiest villages in Britain, to castles high on wild hilltops or coastal crags, to remote valleys and islands where monks once built their monasteries, and to busy cities where Norman houses still lie hidden among the modern buildings, and cathedrals offer quiet sanctuaries from the traffic. Understandably, some of the buildings are in ruin or altered after eight or more centuries, but there are great riches to discover and enjoy in the mysteries of the surviving Anglo-Saxon churches, the mighty carved high crosses, in the changing designs of massive keeps and small stone houses, the sonorous spaces of early Norman abbeys and the outburst of ornate Romanesque sculpture in Anglo-Norman churches from about 1130 until the period ends before 1200 with the Transitional buildings developing into the Gothic style of the thirteenth century.

The buildings of this era include the earliest after Britain started to emerge from the chaotic period following the withdrawal of the Romans in about AD 410. The style of these buildings has caused much argument among architectural historians: are they close enough to the style prevalent in continental Europe throughout these centuries to be classed as Romanesque, or not? In general, I have chosen to call the Anglo-Norman buildings Romanesque, but not their wayward Celtic and Anglo-Saxon predecessors.

Romanesque is a term generally used to describe all the variants of a style prevailing in western Europe (from Italy to Scandinavia, and from East Germany to lowland Scotland) between the end of the Roman Empire in the sixth century and the rise of the Gothic style around 1200. Romanesque architecture was derived and developed far from Roman design: it is characterised by solid walls, flat or tunnel-vaulted or groin-vaulted roofs, round-topped arches, capitals that reject Classical discipline, and massive piers. The Anglo-Norman buildings in Britain are part of this wider western European Romanesque tradition, while most of the earlier works have a more vernacular character as well as varying degrees of continental Romanesque and even Byzantine influence.

The buildings of the centuries before the Conquest of 1066 fall into two distinct periods. From 600 until 800 there are the early churches of Kent, Northumbria and Mercia – the kingdoms that emerged in that order – plus one in Essex. The foundations of houses and simple royal palaces of that time have been excavated, but apart from the churches, one possibly Anglian tower at York is the only survivor in three dimensions. Building materials in use then were wood, re-used Roman bricks and rather roughly dressed stone. The architectural styles in Kent were drawn from the Continent, as were the more northerly churches to a lesser degree. Their spatial achievement is high. Among other monuments, the tall stone crosses and a few monasteries in Scotland are impressive.

Then came the century of Viking raids throughout the 800s and little seems to have been built during those years. The great flowering of late Anglo-Saxon building follows from c. 900 until 1066. Of the 300 or so known sites with Anglo-Saxon remains, several dozen are substantial and rewarding to visit. Most of them are churches, a few are monastery ruins. The building materials were again chiefly timber and stone. The styles show links with the Carolingian Empire's Romanesque, though native English features emerge in some quite ambitious structures. Architectural detailing remained simple and rather rough, though often powerfully expressive. Sculpture fluctuated a great deal in quality, sometimes showing real if naïve refinement.

With the Conquest, all that changed. In the period up to about 1100, the early cathedrals, churches and castles show the fierce discipline of spaces and lack of ornament typical of contemporary Romanesque work in Normandy. Any sculpture that appears is inept. Stone is the only surviving building material, though most castles and houses were of wood. Masonry is rough ashlar or sometimes of the herringbone pattern that may have appeared in Britain well before the Conquest. Most of the major cathedrals were started at this time, though little of this earliest Norman architecture has survived later rebuildings.

During the reign of Henry I, the peaceful period from 1100 to 1135, spaces became more open and carving more able, though the architecture was still generally concerned with simple grand forms. But at Durham cathedral, rib-vaulting, great drum-piers and zigzag ornament appeared and were taken up elsewhere. The Romanesque was imported to southern Wales by Norman settlers and to lowland Scotland, introduced by the Norman-educated King David I.

The years 1135–54 were politically turbulent in England, as

The most widespread motifs of late Norman architectural carving – scalloped capitals, zigzag and beakhead – at Stewkley church, Buckinghamshire (c. 1140–50)

powerful barons fought each other under a weak king. Yet this was the time when a great renaissance of architectural decoration started, with new ornamental motifs and richly sculpted arches spreading through the abbeys and parish churches of the south. In the north, in contrast, the new Cistercian monasteries introduced their simplified architectural forms and pointed arches together with rounded ones.

Finally, the rest of the century saw both these trends – the enriching and the simplifying – fulfilled. The great cathedrals were completed. Order was re-established by Henry II and some of his many castles reflect radical architectural ideas brought home by Crusaders. In the countryside some local lords moved from small wooden castles to small stone manor-houses, while in towns a few wealthy men built stone houses too – the earliest surviving houses are of this time. In churches the schools of decorative Romanesque sculpture produced much magnificent work, although the simple Cistercian features and structural advances spread too. And at Canterbury, real Gothic appears from 1175 onwards, in preparation for the end of the Romanesque around 1200.

Most of the architectural features and ornamental motifs of the period are illustrated in the photographs and identified in the captions or text in the following chapters. But the Glossary and the diagram below indicating the usual names used for the parts of the Romanesque arch may be found useful for reference.

Simplified diagram of a Romanesque arch, showing the names usually given to the constituent parts

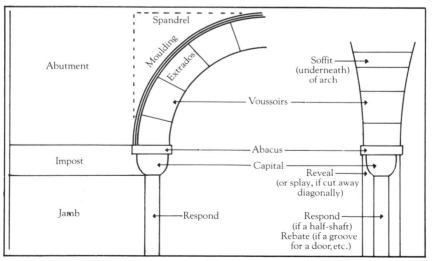

Seen from outside the arch   Seen from under the arch

1

ANGLO-SAXON AND CELTIC BUILDINGS AND CROSSES

The Anglo-Saxon and other peoples who occupied Britain between AD 500 and 1066 have left a scattered sample of their works – mostly churches, little monasteries and high crosses – charged with a special magic. That magic arises partly from the remoteness of many sites – remoteness in time as well as location around these islands – from our scant knowledge of the people who built and used them, and from the sheer strangeness of their sense of architectural beauty and ways of life to us who rediscover them for ourselves. Gradually one sorts out in one's mind where the remains of early Celtic missionaries, St Augustine's followers, and the Saxon kingdoms of England fit into a time span of 500 years, and comes to see that there were two main architectural periods – from 600 to 800, and then, after a century of Viking destruction, from 900 to 1066 with increasing continental Romanesque influence. Both periods have left many fragmentary remains of considerable aesthetic achievement and evocative mystery, an English vernacular in moving contrast to the disciplined magnificence of Norman Romanesque.

The Saxons, whom the Romanised Britons invited to defend the south against Scottish raiders in about 420, had themselves long plundered and settled the south-eastern coasts: a series of immense Roman fortresses still punctuates this 'Saxon Shore'. But these mercenaries from the north-west German coast turned on their hosts. In the words of a British monk, Gildas, written a century later, they became a fire burning Britain 'until it scorched nearly the whole area of the island and licked the western seas with its savage red tongue'. From 450 onwards the Saxons started to settle most of south and central England, attracting other tribes to take land in modern Surrey (Franks), in parts of Kent (Jutes), in smaller pockets (Frisians and Suebians), and all up the eastern side from Suffolk to Northumberland and Edinburgh (Angles). The British resistance movements by Ambrosius and Arthur around 500 are famous, but by 550 the great future Anglo-Saxon kingdoms were emerging as the surviving Britons came to accept their more powerful neighbours everywhere, or fled to Wales and Cornwall. It is estimated that England was still peopled by over half a million Britons at this time, compared with at most 100,000 Anglo-Saxon settlers. While the Angles brought their whole families, it seems that many Saxons killed British men and took their womenfolk.

At this time, Gildas tells us, 'the towns of this land are still not inhabited as in old times – they are neglected, much in ruins and deserted'. The newcomers who had slaughtered so many Britons were indeed ferocious, but they were also able farmers who avoided the Romanised town dwellings. There are extremely few shreds of knowledge about their religious views, other than their general Teutonic pantheon of Woden

Great Britain in early Anglo-Saxon times (c. 750)

Great Britain in late Anglo-Saxon times (c. 950), with England under the overlordship of Wessex

et al. and their north-south graves with grave-goods, for Christianity ruthlessly exterminated all records.

It was the pagan Aethelbert's Saxon and Jutish kingdom of Kent which was the first to take form in the 560s. Other warriors were still battling with their fellow chiefs to form Northumbria, from the Humber the width of northern England and up to the Firth of Forth, by 620, Mercia, from the Mersey to the northern side of the Thames, well before 700, and then the southern Saxon kingdoms united by Wessex by 800. And Christianity marched with this political consolidation, seemingly the most important civilising force of the time.

The earliest Christian building in Britain may be the excavated walls of the Casa Candida (White House) church built at Whithorn, Dumfries and Galloway, in c. 400 by St Ninian, a Romano-British missionary bishop who converted many of the southern Picts. Other later monuments by Ninian's successors are located on the relevant map and listed in the Gazetteer. St Patrick had planted a flourishing Romano-British Christianity in Ireland in 405 just as the Empire died, and an Irish prince known as Columba brought the faith back to Britain in 563. In the Inner Hebrides of Scotland, St Columba's main missionary base at Iona still has the traces of a simple cell, said to be his, near its later buildings. But on an almost unreachable and uninhabited isle to the south, an adventurous traveller can still visit extensive remains of Columba's second monastery, Eilach-an-Naoimh; and in Skye another tiny monastic settlement has been revealed at Chaluim Chille in the dried-out bed of a loch. The Deerness monastery on Orkney was a more considerable settlement, with the ruins of a chapel and twenty monks' dwellings in a strong cashel-wall, built from early Christian times well on into the 1100s.

The other branch of Christianity, direct from Rome itself, arrived in Kent while the Celtic Church in Scotland was spreading its missionary outposts down to Lindisfarne in the Anglian kingdom of Northumbria. In the 580s Aethelbert of Kent made contact with the great King Clovis of the Franks, a Christian, and married his daughter Bertha. The Frankish princess brought her chaplain with her to live in Aethelbert's capital, Canterbury. St Martin's Church on the hill outside that city was Bertha's place of worship and the present west and chancel walls, with a square-headed *porticus* entrance (which may have been that of a late Roman church), were part of her

church where St Augustine first prayed at Canterbury. For Aethelbert, doubtless spurred by his queen, willingly if fearfully received the mission sent by Pope Gregory the Great in 597. Augustine, too, was worried, the great historian Bede recorded a century later, about this 'fierce and unbelieving' land. He led his monks chanting across the chalk downs from the coast to Canterbury in full Roman splendour of vestments and carrying silver crosses, which must have astonished the prospering but humble Saxo-Jute farmers they passed. The Italian was received by Aethelbert outside his dwelling in case he cast dangerous spells, but they took to each other and the king was soon converted and granting land for a monastery near his wife's church.

The site of St Augustine's monastery at the foot of St Martin's Hill, outside the walls of Canterbury, is one of the most evocative of this period. For reasons perhaps to do with ancient beliefs about the sacredness of an east-west line (Christian churches have always been aligned east-west, even when built due north of the Holy Land, as were many prehistoric chambered barrows and temple-mountains or pyramids all over the world), Augustine in 597–c. 605 built his chief church, St Peter and St Paul, due west of Bertha's St

The earliest Anglo-Saxon building, in the kingdom of Kent: the blocked doorways to two vanished *porticus*, St Martin's Church, St Martin's Hill, outside Canterbury. The doorway on the left was probably that of Queen Bertha's church, already built when St Augustine arrived and prayed here in 597. The arch on the right is later, perhaps of c. 700

Martin's. Along the same east-west line, Aethelbert's successor added in c. 620 St Mary's Church immediately to the east of St Peter and St Paul, and a little later St Pancras' Church was built still further to the east. Two prehistoric standing stones can be seen at the western end of this line of churches, and a large mound rises nearby, confirming that St Augustine sensibly adopted a place already venerated.

The traces of the churches, however – of which only St Martin's and St Pancras' have early walls still standing – show that Augustine brought Italian ideas about church architecture. He had been the prior of a Benedictine monastery in Rome. This was the earliest major monastic order by a margin of nearly six centuries (see Chapter 5), founded at Monte Cassino, north of Naples, in 529 by St Benedict and later widened to give organised form to the increasing number of hermit communities. Obedience, poverty, chastity, peace, manual labour and the civilised arts were Benedict's 'rule' in a period of chaos. And Augustine brought these ideas with him to a land itself just emerging from such violent times. Among his thirty monks there must have been designers and craftsmen, for the great scholar Sir Alfred Clapham has shown that Augustine's churches in Canterbury are influenced by what were then fairly recent churches in and around Ravenna and in Constantinople, as well as by those around Naples (Nola) and Rome itself.

The plans of these churches, still traceable at Canterbury, show aisleless naves and apsed chancels – simplified from the classic basilica plan of very early Christian architecture (with its aisled nave, with rows of columns between nave and aisles, clerestory windows above, and at its eastern end a chancel or presbytery with a semi-circular half-domed apse for the altar).

Rather curiously, apses were not being built in new churches in Rome in the late 500s, but they were in Byzantine Ravenna and nearby Pomposa. The eastern origin of the monk-mason or architect responsible for the Kent churches is confirmed by the triple-arched openings between nave and chancel; not done through structural ineptitude, but to symbolise the Trinity, to screen the sanctity of the chancel (where only priests could go) and to dramatise the way the three-dimensional spaces connect with each other.

Another feature shared by these Kent churches is the *porticus*, a mysterious feature in many late Anglo-Saxon churches too. *Porticus* is a plural word which means literally a pair of little porches, but among Anglo-Saxon builders came

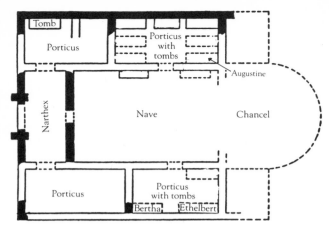

Plans of three of the early churches aligned east-west at Canterbury (starting with St Peter and St Paul in the west)

St Peter and St Paul (597-c.605)

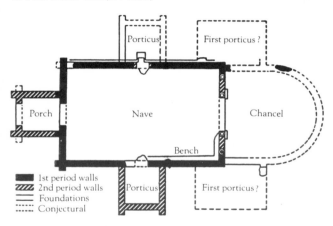

1st period walls
2nd period walls
Foundations
Conjectural

St Pancras (probably c. 630)

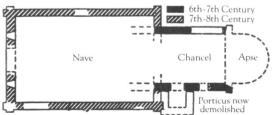

6th-7th Century
7th-8th Century

St Martin (parts pre-597, other walls 7th and 8th centuries)

N

to mean small chambers with low doorways and roofs, opening off the nave, the chancel, or later, off the space under a tower. They were probably derived from the Diaconicon (for keeping the Communion vessels, so opening off the chancel) and the Prothesis (for receiving lay-people's offerings before presenting them at the altar, so opening off the nave) of the eastern Church in the 500s, and from the Cubicula (for important burials and for lay-people's meditation) off the nave of a major church near Naples of c. 400. At Augustine's church of St Peter and St Paul there were apparently two *porticus* off the chancel (perhaps for the vessels and a vestry), and two more off the nave for the tombs of Augustine himself and his five successor abbots and, on the south, for Aethelbert and Bertha. Later, a *narthex*, or porch open on the entrance side, was added at the west end and two more *porticus* on either side, so that the main Canterbury church consisted of a series of spaces coming to a climax in the apse behind the triple-arched opening.

Similar features can be seen in the more substantial Roman brick ruins of the third new church at Canterbury, St Pancras' (the second new church of St Mary was almost obliterated by later additions), and the visible remains of all these four aligned buildings are described in the Gazetteer. The features appeared again in the other Kent churches built during the 600s by Augustine's disciples. These were St Andrew's Church, Rochester, c. 604 (vanished, but the plan has been excavated), St Mary, Lyminge (the foundations of Bertha's daughter St Aethelburga's mixed-sex priory church of c. 633 have been excavated, and the church has many late Anglo-Saxon features visible in its generally much rebuilt structure), and St Mary, Reculver (c. 670, destroyed as recently as 1809, but the plan is visible from the foundations: a nave with triple-arched apsed chancel and six *porticus*, beside the surviving Norman towers). The final church of St Augustine's seventh-century group was built by St Cedd, whom Aethelbert sent to convert his relative king of the East Saxons in c. 655. More remains of this than of the others, for by a happy chance the nave was used as a farmer's barn until quite recently. This is St Peter, Bradwell-juxta-Mare, Essex, and in its simple preserved walls can be seen traces of its former west porch, east apse and *porticus* openings, one into the nave, the other into the chancel (as well as the larger openings later made for farm carts).

Away from the south-east there are surviving churches of the 600s in two other Anglo-Saxon kingdoms: seven in

Northumbria, and at least one – the finest of all – in Mercia, though most of them are fragmentary.

In c. 627 the monk Paulinus, a Roman sent by Augustine, stood 'black-haired, thin-faced, aquiline-nosed, venerable and awe-inspiring of appearance' before the council of King Edwin of Northumbria near Goodmanham in Yorkshire (now Humberside). The kingdom had been recently formed and after one old man had made the famous comparison of life without religious vision to 'a sparrow's flight through a firelit hall where one sits feasting in winter … in at one opening, a moment in the light and warmth, then flying out at another door and disappearing into the winter night', Christianity was adopted. The only remains of Edwin's time are the excavated foundations of his palace complex (not viewable now) at Yeavering, Northumberland, and perhaps the Anglian Tower visible among the Roman walls of York.

Edwin did not live to spread the new religion far, but his successors did. Under the influence of St Wilfrid, abbot and later Bishop of York, the advancing Celtic Church and its beatific St Cuthbert of Lindisfarne were outmanoeuvred by the Roman faction of Canterbury during a great debate in 664 – the Synod of Whitby. A new and brilliant Archbishop of Canterbury, Theodore of Tarsus, then encouraged his English abbot Benedict Biscop to found two famous monasteries at Monkwearmouth in c. 675 and Jarrow (home of the Venerable Bede, the great historian, for the following four decades) in c. 685.

The remains at Monkwearmouth, solitary now in the middle of industrial Sunderland, are the tall slim tower and some other fragments. But there is enough to give a vivid idea of the early church. Its porch survives as the base of the tower and main entrance, with the curious baluster-shafts (cylindrical with band decoration only) and some primitive carving. The proportions of the nave can be seen too, tall and narrow, like a swift path up to salvation for the spirit.

At Jarrow, now in a prime example of an environmental waste-land, the original church of St Paul was in ruins by Victorian times and was replaced by the present nave. But the eminent authority on Anglo-Saxon architecture, Dr H. M. Taylor, has pointed out that Bede records three churches there, probably aligned east-west as at Canterbury. Taylor concludes that the present chancel, with its obviously early Anglo-Saxon masonry and windows, was the St Mary's Church (of perhaps the 690s) mentioned by Bede and

Right: The chancel wall of Jarrow abbey church, Benedict Biscop's second Northumbrian foundation, c. 685, and the monastery of the Venerable Bede. The present chancel was probably St Mary's Church, c. 690, one of three small separate churches aligned east-west

Below: In the Anglian kingdom of Northumbria, Monkwearmouth abbey church, near the centre of Sunderland. The lower part of the tower was built for Benedict Biscop as a two-storey porch in c. 675, the upper tower in c. 990

probably joined to the first church in later Anglo-Saxon times (although the top of the resulting central tower is early Norman). There are extensive Anglo-Saxon monastery remains around the church, their main date of perhaps c. 1030 indicated by one of the triangular-headed doorways so much enjoyed at that time.

Another Northumbrian church is that of Escomb, a small gem of c. 680. It sits today in a council housing-estate in a remote County Durham hamlet and is ill-signposted. But, with the exception of a few later windows cut for daylight, it is intact; it has good Anglian stonework, an undecorated nave with *porticus*, a square chancel, and a fine simple chancel arch that may be re-used Roman. Again, the nave is long and tall for its width, immediately suggestive of pure austere godliness.

At Hexham in modern Northumberland and Ripon in North Yorkshire, the later fine churches (see Gazetteer) are built above extraordinary crypts of stone covered with iron-hard Anglian cement, both built by St Wilfrid in c. 680 to enshrine and show to pilgrims the saints' bones that he brought back from Rome (these have gone now). Finally of these early northern churches, the porch, tower arch and part of the nave of St Andrew's, Corbridge, are of c. 780, re-using Roman building material. The porch is now blocked and forms the lower part of the Norman tower, but the proportions of the remains show that here again was one of the high, narrow and long naves typical of Northumbria at that time. Despite the influence of Canterbury, the Northumbrian chancels seem all to have been small and square, with no apses and none of the triple-arched chancel openings of Augustine's Kent.

One of those Kent churches, at Reculver, had a high stone cross in front of its triple-arched chancel. Fragments of that

Escomb church in County Durham, c. 680. The walls are original, as are some minute windows high up. The taller windows are medieval, inserted to admit more daylight

Interior of Escomb church, with the original chancel arch and tall narrow proportions of c. 680; the windows shown here were enlarged later

cross survive and show a delicate carving of drapery far beyond anything achieved by English craftsmen. The hands that carved it were probably those of a monk from the Mediterranean, trained in sculpture. But the Reculver cross is the only one known in the south-east. Elsewhere in Britain, such crosses can be seen in or just outside many village churches.

Many explanations for these crosses have been put forward. One theory is that when missionaries made converts in a village, they would put up a wooden cross as a gathering-place for prayers. In time this might have been replaced by one of the carved stone crosses, and then perhaps a wooden chapel built where there would be a stone church centuries later. Whatever the true explanation, there seems no doubt that the Northumbrian Christians adopted the Celtic Church's custom of high crosses. Many simple standing stones inscribed with crosses or Pictish symbols can be seen in Scotland and other Celtic lands. Dating is difficult but from the late 600s the stones are dressed, if roughly, and carved with occasional figures and interlace patterns in addition to the cross or symbols of Pictdom; their kingdom, centred around Perth and north of it, has many stones to show. Moreover, the crosses around St Ninian's Whithorn may mean that accomplished examples date back nearer to his time.

The Scottish crosses reach a peak with the art of the 'Scotic' (Irish Scots) kingdom of Dalriada (Argyll and around it), those in Iona and Islay of the late 900s being best-known. In Cornwall and parts of Wales the custom existed too, and there are good examples here. There are a number in the Midlands (Mercia) but above all they are widespread in northern

The shaft of a sculpted cross, perhaps of the 800s, at Meifod in Powys, Wales. The carving includes crucifixus, ornate cross, interlace and other Celtic motifs

England (Northumbria). The famous Bewcastle and Ruthwell crosses in the north-west probably date from the 680s and may well reflect the arrival of a foreign craftsman, perhaps with Benedict Biscop, after Rome's triumph at the Synod of Whitby. The crosses marked on the maps will be found to date from all periods up to c. 1100, with many rises and falls in the standard of carving. Their motifs include vine tendrils and interlace adapted from the Italian, diagonal fretwork like multiple key-pattern, checkers, pelta and trumpet-spiral. In Cheshire (Mercia) the marvellous Sandbach crosses (now headless) on their step-pyramid bases are of c. 750, while those at Bakewell and Eyam in Derbyshire are a little later.

Celtic cross, probably of the 900s, at Cardinham church, Cornwall

If the remains of seventh-century crosses and churches are rarer in Mercia than in Northumbria, it is because Mercia's great period came later. Throughout the 700s Mercia was the dominant Anglo-Saxon kingdom. Its King Offa built a mighty dike or ditched earth wall almost the length of the Welsh border to protect one side of his realm. Within it he founded a number of planned towns, and at its eastern side he fought the East Anglians in the marshes of Cambridgeshire. He was also overlord of London and built a new shrine for the saint at St Albans.

Within Mercia's borders lies the greatest of all the surviving Anglo-Saxon churches of the 600s, the abbey church of Brixworth, now in Northamptonshire. What is seen today is the greater part of the building done in c. 675 by monks from Peterborough (a two-storey entrance porch, a long arcaded nave running on into a square chancel, then a narrower apse) but now without the aisles and *porticus* that ran on both sides of the nave, and with the following later alterations. In about 790 an underground crypt was built around the outside of the apse, in a curve like an ambulatory, presumably for pilgrims to view holy relics. During the 900s the church, partly in ruins, had the apse rebuilt, the aisles and *porticus* demolished, the arcade arches blocked to become the present church walls, and the

In the Anglo-Saxon kingdom of Mercia, Brixworth church, Northamptonshire, the great abbey church of c. 675; the wide nave, chancel and, beyond the arch of re-used Roman bricks, the apse

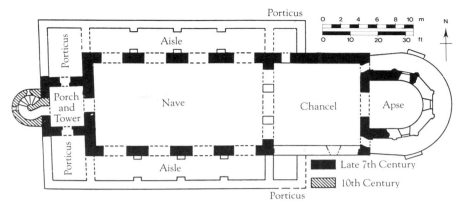

Above: Brixworth church, Northamptonshire (c. 675, with later alterations; aisles and *porticus* now destroyed)

Right: The mysterious west wall of Brixworth church nave. The lower part of the tower was a two-storey porch (c. 675) with two openings to the nave (one the blocked upper arch seen here). This porch was extended upwards as the present tower during the 900s, when the triple opening to the tower room was added

porch extended upwards to become a tower with a new round stair turret against it (which explains the high blocked arch on the west wall inside the nave). The battlements, the spire, the south chapel and many other windows were added much later in medieval history. But the majestic white nave, with its round arcade arches and clerestory of narrow Roman tiles, is the masterpiece of surviving early Anglo-Saxon spatial design.

Brixworth serves as witness (perhaps with the early naves of the churches in Wing in Buckinghamshire and Deerhurst in Gloucestershire) for the many great churches built in Mercia in the 700s – cathedrals at Worcester, Lichfield and Leicester, abbeys at St Albans, Peterborough, Ely and elsewhere. Some taste of the Mercian achievement may be had from the finely sculpted stones preserved in the walls of Breedon-on-the-Hill church in Leicestershire, although the church itself is a rebuilding of the 1300s.

Apart from later rebuilding, the reason the great early churches have disappeared is that the end of the 700s saw the start of the Viking devastation of England and the gradual destruction of Mercia by these Norse invaders. In a passage ironically echoing Gildas's description of the Saxons in 450, another monk (descended from those Saxons) called Alcuin describes the Vikings around 800: 'The attacks of the pagans tragically destroyed God's church in Lindisfarne with plunder and killing. Behold St Cuthbert's church splashed with the blood of God's priests, stripped and burned.' The Danes and Norwegians returned year after year for decades destroying and robbing the coastal settlements, then sailing up rivers to land small armies. Brixworth is close to the geographical centre of England, but by 870 it was one of countless churches in scorched ruin. By then the Danes had settled in large numbers throughout eastern England. They would have had the rest if Alfred had not rallied the Saxons of Wessex, held the Norse to the line of Watling Street by 890, and then founded a kingdom that would soon take back overlord control of all English land for a century, including the eastern parts called the Danelaw.

Alfred, King of Wessex, tamer of the Vikings and founder of a minster at Winchester (his queen founded a third church there), a monastery at Athelney and a score of *burhs* (fortified towns), has left no building certainly traceable to his reign of 871–99. Of the early 800s, before the worst of the Viking devastation, there are important church remains at Britford (Wiltshire), Titchfield (Hampshire), Bishopstone (East Sussex), Hackness (North Yorkshire) and Bardsey (West

Relief sculpture panel of Christ (c. 800) in the Mercian style of Peterborough, one of many Anglo-Saxon carvings in Breedon-on-the-Hill church, Leicestershire

Yorkshire), and probably the little monastery and chapel at Heysham (Lancashire). After that there is nothing substantial (for the long-halled palace of King Edward the Elder of c. 900, excavated at Cheddar, Somerset, was of timber) until the renaissance of the 900s.

During that century the basic structure of the English village and countryside, with its differing social systems in the eastern Danelaw and the western Anglo-Saxon area, was established. The Saxon social structure consisted of slaves, ceorls (free peasants with their own land), gesiths or ealdormen or thanes

St Patrick's monastery chapel, probably of the 800s, overlooking the sea at Heysham, Lancashire. The grooved moulding of the arch is extremely unusual

Excavated plans of royal palaces. King Edwin of Northumbria's Yeavering (c. 616–32) and the later kings of Wessex's Cheddar (c. 900 and second stage c. 1000)

(lords owning land for at least five cattle), and the great lords, local kings or eorls under the king himself. In the Danelaw the system simply consisted of freemen and local lords. The early Saxon system of justice by blood-feud had been gradually replaced by that of *wergild*, a man's price for fine or recompense; this ranged from 200 Wessex shillings for a ceorl, to 600 for a gesith and double that for a great lord. From the Danelaw, the custom of twelve-freemen juries was introduced. Locally, there were folk-moots and the king's representative, later the shire-reeve or sheriff.

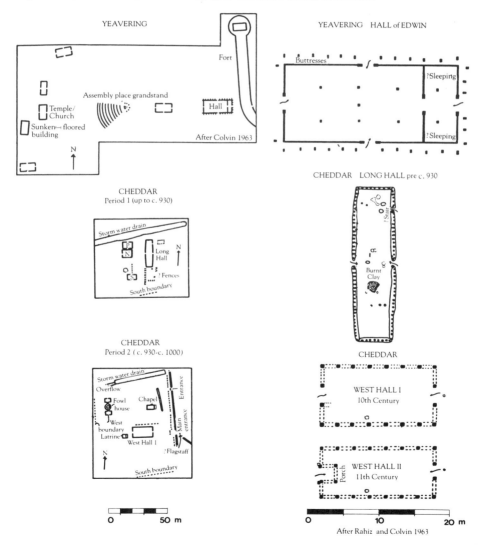

YEAVERING

Fort

Assembly place grandstand

Temple/Church

Sunken–floored building

Hall

N

After Colvin 1963

YEAVERING HALL of EDWIN

Buttresses

?Sleeping

?Sleeping

CHEDDAR
Period 1 (up to c. 930)

Storm water drain

Long Hall

N

? Fences

South boundary

CHEDDAR LONG HALL pre c. 930

?Stair

Burnt Clay

CHEDDAR
Period 2 (c. 930–c. 1000)

Storm water drain

Overflow

Fowl house

Chapel

West boundary

Latrine

West Hall 1

N

?Flagstaff

South boundary

Entrance

Main entrance

CHEDDAR

WEST HALL I
10th Century

WEST HALL II
11th Century

Porch

0   50 m

0   10   20 m

After Rahiz and Colvin 1963

Left: St Mary's Church at Deerhurst, Gloucestershire. The original Mercian church of perhaps c. 790 was enlarged, destroyed by Vikings and then rebuilt in c. 930 and later, when this western end of the nave was altered as the two-storey porch was heightened into a tower. Triangular-headed arches are a late Anglo-Saxon feature

Below: Deerhurst church. The north 'transept', originally *porticus*, with a late Saxon triangular-topped doorway and other openings in the exposed stonework

At some time in the increasingly prosperous tenth century, with Archbishops Oda and Dunstan presiding over a religious revival from Canterbury in 950–90, two of the finest monuments of Anglo-Saxon architecture took something like their present form. Perhaps the loveliest of all is Deerhurst church in Mercian Gloucestershire. Like Brixworth, it went through several stages from a simple nave and apsed chancel building of perhaps c. 790 to a surrounding complex of *porticus* with a western porch. It was then destroyed by Vikings during the 800s and rebuilt in c. 930 with the tower above the porch, a new chancel arch and the now-ruined apse. The tall white interior, some parts now with the rough stone exposed, is given added mystery by doorways and other apertures of various building periods in the aisles and high up the walls.

The nave at Wing in Buckinghamshire may be as old as that of Brixworth. But Mercia's power had gone by 900 and its polygonal apsed chancel was rebuilt around 950 by the Lady Aelfgifu of the Wessex royal family. This apse, with its vaulted crypt beneath, contains features that became typical in the large number of surviving Anglo-Saxon churches built in c. 1020–66, when Cnut (or Canute) had re-established a peaceful kingdom following his father Sweyn's destructive raids from Denmark and conquest of 994–1013.

The apse of the 900s (crypt below) added to the early Mercian nave of Wing church, Buckinghamshire. The slender pilaster-strips, or lesenes, became a favourite Anglo-Saxon feature, as did the blank arcades (the large windows are medieval additions) and the triangular forms above

The exterior of the apse at Wing (the interior has been altered) is decorated with blank arcading and the so-called pilaster-strips or lesenes (a word derived from the Carolingian Rhineland features which an early authority, Professor Baldwin Brown, believed to be their source). At Wing they are formed from the protruding ends of stones running deep into the wall, but in their widespread later form they are usually long strips of stone embedded quite shallowly in the strong cement surface.

At the top of the Wing pilaster-strips, the upper blank arcade shows another typical late Anglo-Saxon feature – the triangular-headed arch. Also at Wing there is one of the splendid wide chancel arches of the late period; here it is very simple, but as the decades moved on towards the Norman Conquest, the forms gradually became more ornamented and moulded until they reached the sophistication of the chancel arch of c. 1060 at Bosham, West Sussex. Most arches remained round-headed, some over very small windows carved from a single stone. Double-splayed windows, cut away at the sides both inside and out to allow more light, became a stock feature.

During the eleventh century the plans of churches came nearer to the European mainstream. The *porticus* grew gradually larger, becoming more like real transepts in churches such as at Breamore, Hampshire (c. 1010), St Mary-in-Castro, Dover (c. 1020) and reaching a full cruciform plan with huge crossing arches at the cathedral-like church of Stow in Lincolnshire (either c. 1010 or c. 1040).

Stonework too had its typical forms. On the outside of the transept of Breamore church and many other buildings there are good examples of the long-and-short work quoins of the early 1000s, corners secured by alternating heavy stones laid

In the Saxon kingdom of Wessex, the south transept of Breamore church, Hampshire, c. 1010. The tall narrow proportions, small window and long-and-short work corners (quoins) are characteristic of late Anglo-Saxon architecture

Left: St Mary's Church at Stow, Lincolnshire. Today it seems just a big parish church, but when built in the early 1000s it was larger than contemporary Anglo-Saxon cathedrals

Below left: The crossing of Stow church, Lincolnshire. The main arches, with massive roll-mouldings and an outer frame, are of typical late Anglo-Saxon (or Anglo-Danish, here in the Danelaw) design, though exceptionally large. The pointed arches within the tower space are medieval, added to strengthen the tower

Right: The chancel arch and chancel, Bradford-on-Avon church, Wiltshire. This notable Wessex church, thought to date from before 1000, is built all of dressed masonry of simple detailing but unusually fine finish for the time

vertically and horizontally. When these stones are particularly huge they are called megalithic. Just before and after the Norman Conquest there was a fashion for masonry laid in herringbone patterns. At St Laurence's in Bradford-on-Avon, Wiltshire (c. 1000 or earlier), the ashlar masonry is of an exceptionally high standard, with well-executed blank arcading all round the outside. At the other extreme, many churches were probably of timber only: the nave of the church at Greensted, Essex (c. 1010), is a unique survivor.

Towers became widespread after 1000, taking various forms. The simplest is the stocky square-plan west tower with tiny windows and larger bell-openings near the top, each of

these almost invariably having a double opening with a fat little column in its centre and in the middle of the thickness of the wall. Hundreds of such towers are still scattered around England, often undetected if their bell-openings were widened later. The reason for their sudden appearance in England in c. 980 is quite simple. The idea of the bell-tower did not exist in Christendom until its appearance in Italy in about 850. None exists in France earlier than c. 950 and its spread is clearly associated with the renewed out-going vigour of the Papacy that reached England under Dunstan in the decades before the second Danish invasions of c. 1000.

These common Anglo-Saxon characteristics can be seen in the famous tower of St Peter's Church, Barton-on-Humber, of c. 990, together with splendid pilaster-strip work, or lesenes, and a durable cemented surface. This tower is one of those that functioned within as the main space or nave of the church – it still has its western forebuilding, though the existing later

Earls Barton church, Northamptonshire. The most elaborate of all the lesene-stripped and blank-arcaded late Anglo-Saxon church towers (c. 1020–50). The plump shafts of the unusual multiple tower openings and the more disciplined long-and-short work quoins are also remarkable

The forebuilding and tower (which served as the nave) of Barton-on-Humber church, Humberside, c. 990. Here the lesenes seen at Wing have developed into strong surface ornament of stones set in cement, with blank arcading round-topped below and triangular-headed above

church to the east swept away its small chancel. But the best example of a tower with pilaster-strip ornament is Earls Barton church, in Northamptonshire, of c. 1020. Here the bell-openings are quintuple, the tower rises in four stages divided by horizontal string-courses, there are arches of several kinds, and the lesenes form vivid patterns reminiscent of timber-work.

A few round staircase turrets added in this period to towers such as those at Brixworth or Broughton (Humberside) are similar to other round church towers of the time. In flint and chalk country, from Sussex to Norfolk, there are many churches with round Anglo-Saxon towers: the church of

Herringbone and megalithic masonry, widespread late Anglo-Saxon features, in the tower and projecting stair turret, c. 1050, of Broughton church, Humberside

Forncett St Peter in Norfolk is an accomplished example of c. 1050. The circular plan was probably to strengthen the structure of flints and cement, which had no shaped masonry stones, though it may have had symbolic meaning too.

Further north there are tall round towers of a very different tradition. At the great Irish monasteries of this time, such as Clonmacnoise and Glendalough, high round towers were fairly common, perhaps built partly as watch-towers against the frequent raiders of the period. Irish Celtic monks may have brought the idea to their brothers in Scotland, though the lofty lower part of the square tower at the great Scottish monastery of Restenneth (founded in c. 710 by Nechtan, King of the

Forncett St Peter church, Norfolk, c. 1050. One of the scores of East Anglian round towers built before and after the Norman Conquest. The bell-opening with one shaft in the thickness of the wall is often seen in round and square church towers of this time

Picts) predates the Irish towers. At any rate, the 86-foot-high tower at Brechin cathedral, Tayside Region, dates from c. 1000 and the entrance high in its side has figure sculpture in the Scottish-Irish tradition. This series of high towers continues in Scotland at least up to the Norman Conquest: at Abernethy, further south, the round tower is of c. 1050 or later and at the initial cathedral of c. 1140 at St Andrews (now St Rule's Church) the tall square tower may be earlier than the little church built east and west of its base.

Most Anglo-Saxon towers are today crowned by additions, parapets or spires added much later. The form their original tops took is not known, but there is good reason to think that many were capped by diagonal steeples of the 'Rhenish Helm' type seen in churches of this time in the Rhineland. Only one English church retains its Anglo-Saxon steeple of this kind, at Sompting in West Sussex, built in perhaps c. 1050. It still seems to perform visual conjuring tricks as one walks around

The round tower of c. 1000 (steeple added later) in the churchyard of Brechin cathedral, Tayside Region. The tower, from an Irish tradition, has seven storeys of timber inside and a doorway with good but eroded Celtic sculpture

The tower of Sompting church, West Sussex, c. 1050, the only one in Britain to retain what may have been a fairly widespread type of early steeple derived from Romanesque churches of the Carolingian Rhineland. The bell-openings and windows are conventional late Anglo-Saxon forms, but the central vertical lesene on each face is unusual

it, the angled facets of the roofs and walls constantly changing their geometrical patterns. Less still is known of the original roofs of the churches themselves – presumably they would all have been thatched.

Inside the church at Sompting (with its mystifying spaces rebuilt later by the Templars) are examples of Saxon architectural stone carving in its last stage. When one considers the heights of craftsmanship reached earlier on the great crosses of the north, the hatching and volutes of the Sompting tower arch capitals seem extraordinarily crude, although they are fair enough representatives of the ordinary level of sculpture in churches around the country at this time. Much more pleasing are five lengths of finely carved intertwined foliage of an earlier period, displayed on the walls and reminders of what could be achieved. It is hard to escape the conclusion that imported crafts were repeatedly taken up with much talent in England, but as in other fields the society lacked the self-discipline that would have led to a sustained refinement of indigenous culture.

By 1050 Norman architecture had already made a beach-head in England, for the pious King Edward had studied in Normandy and brought Norman craftsmen to build his new Westminster Abbey, now vanished. Of the Confessor's abbey only the caricature in the Bayeux tapestry is known, but with the five Norman bishops he set over English sees, his big Norman-style church seems an ironic pre-echo of the engulfing of Anglo-Saxon culture in 1066.

Suggestions for Travellers

Apart from the major examples already mentioned, late Anglo-Saxon churches of particular interest and complete-ness can be seen at Worth (West Sussex), Repton (Derbyshire), Canford Magna (Dorset), Great Paxton (Cambridgeshire) and Dunham Magna (Norfolk). The maps also make it clear that groups of Anglo-Saxon churches well worth visiting can be found in Kent; along the Sussex-Hampshire coast; in western Hampshire, Wiltshire and Berkshire; in western Oxfordshire and Gloucestershire; in Shropshire; in central and north-west Essex; in northern Northamptonshire and Cambridgeshire; in northern Suffolk and eastern Norfolk; in northern Lincolnshire and Humberside; north and east of Leeds; in Cleveland and south Durham; and in Northumberland. An enjoyable day can be spent travelling around any one of these areas.

2

NORMAN CASTLES

Anglo-Saxon England suffered much from invasions by the Norsemen of Denmark and Norway in the 800s and again around 1000. In 1066 another branch of these people, who had taken north-west France from the Franks in 910 and built an almost independent Norse dukedom, finally took over the prosperous English kingdom. There is often an absurd aspect to invasions, in the small numbers needed for success if the invaders have superior tactics. In this case, 10 major barons, 160 lesser lords, about 1,500 Norman and French knights, and between 5,000 and 8,000 soldiers, mostly mercenaries – under 10,000 in all – simply took control of a sizeable country and its people numbering, according to recent estimates, almost two million. They met with resistance in one major battle in which most of the English gesiths were killed; in a few stands by the remaining Anglo-Saxon lords; in one major insurrection in the north; and doubtless in innumerable local confrontations with individual freemen unrecorded by history books.

The Norman tactics were to use their horsemen against people on foot and simply to kill everyone who resisted. And it does seem that the population dropped considerably in the villages and *burhs* around the country just after the Conquest. Then William paid off the mercenary troops and sent them home before dividing up most of the dead Anglo-Saxons' properties between 170 Norman leaders; they in turn gave sub-lettings to about 1,500 of their followers.

William's strategy in dividing the land was far-sighted. Instead of giving whole shires to his great barons, so creating big geographical properties that would make the lords too powerful for their ruler's security, he gave each of these magnates a number of smaller estates in many parts of England. Thus Henry de Ferrers, later Earl of Derby, was given small numbers of Anglo-Saxon estates in each of Hampshire, Wiltshire, Gloucestershire, Herefordshire, Oxfordshire, Buckinghamshire, Nottinghamshire and Essex, with 8 estates in Staffordshire, 20 in Berkshire, 35 in Leicestershire and 114 in Derbyshire. Only in troubled border country, such as Cornwall, East Anglia (always in danger of invasion by Norway) and the Welsh Marches did he give big areas to barons related or close to him. He also gave one quarter of all the land to the Church and kept one fifth for the Crown, his royal forests and his immediate family. By the time the Domesday Book was compiled as a record of taxable estates in England in 1086, twenty Norman magnates held a quarter of all the country as tenants-in-chief to the king. Only two of the roughly 1,700 landowners of any size were still English, and the smallholders who had controlled most of the land virtually disappeared except in the Danelaw.

Once allotted their estates in exchange for taxes and undertaking to supply a named number of knights, the Norman landowners moved swiftly from county to county securing their properties. This was done largely by the building

Totnes Castle, Devon. The motte and bailey earthworks are of c. 1070, with the timber shell-keep on the motte rebuilt in stone in c. 1200

of thousands of simple forts with small garrisons, the so-called motte-and-bailey castles. There was no Anglo-Saxon tradition of castle building (the *burhs* had been towns with earth and timber defences), and the Normans seem to have developed the type afresh for building cheaply and fast on their many scattered estates. In each, the Saxon peasants were put to work digging a large mound (motte) of earth, with ditches and banks around a wider enclosure (bailey) beside the hillock. None of the early buildings at these fortresses survives, for the tower or keep on the motte, and the strong fences or palisades on the bailey's bank, were of timber. But over 3,000 earthen mottes can still be seen in the English countryside, many of them with their bailey earthworks still there. Thus, with a network of military outpost after outpost across the country, the land was politically gripped.

As time went on some of the timber structures were replaced by stone and this usually produced a castle of the type called a shell-keep on top of the motte. Early examples include royal shell-keeps at Lincoln and the outer ring of the Round Tower at Windsor, both of c. 1110; later ones are at Arundel, in West Sussex, and Carisbrooke, on the Isle of Wight, of c. 1130, while the West Country stone shell-keeps at Totnes, Launceston and Cardiff are of c. 1200.

Shell-keeps usually consist of circular walls, with a single gateway and a sentry-walk around the parapet. In the unroofed area within the shell-keep, wooden buildings were constructed against the wall for use in case of attack, and at Restormel in Cornwall these, unusually, were in time replaced by a stone living hall, chapel and other rooms. The more comfortable dwelling quarters, for peaceful times, including quite ambitious first-floor Great Halls, were built in the less defended area of the inner bailey.

The king himself and the great barons built much more ambitious castles than these, though again their designers' thinking was based on the single defensive stone tower for crises, magnified hugely, with a spacious open enclosure for normal life, where various domestic buildings could provide all the home comforts available in the late eleventh century. At Richmond Castle, North Yorkshire, enough remains of the grand two-storey stone Hall of c. 1080 – on the far side of the bailey from the Norman keep – to give a clear idea of the harsh splendour in which the magnates lived. Remnants of other such Halls are at Tintagel, Cornwall (c. 1145, with its chapel), Eynsford, Kent and Manorbier, Dyfed.

The White Tower, Tower of London, c. 1078–97: William I's hall-keep, with the chapel wing projecting in a curve on the right. The roofs of the turrets and enlarged windows were later alterations

William I, that short thickset warrior of implacable appearance and dictatorial efficiency, settled early on Westminster as his residence when he was in London, though in fact he was in his Norman dukedom for most of his reign as King of England, and travelling around his realm when he was here. It is not known whether he added to the Hall that Edward the Confessor had built near his new abbey, but his son William II, Rufus, built in 1095–7 a timber Westminster Hall that covered the same breathtaking area as the existing Hall (of 1400) beside the Houses of Parliament. Rufus's Hall, its aisles and nave divided by great wooden pillars, was painted all over inside with red and blue 'designs' outlined in black.

The symbol of the king's power in London was of course his castle, rather than his palace. The city's Roman walls still stood at this time and in the corner where these abutted the Thames nearest the sea, the Conqueror at once built a fortified enclosure and presumably a timber tower. In c. 1078, twelve years after the Conquest, he started the present White Tower, the lofty hall-keep that is still the core of the Tower of London. Earlier, in c. 1071, he had started the even larger hall-keep at Colchester, Essex, presumably as a strategic centre for the defence of that flank of England open to another Norse aggressor, for he felt it necessary to raise a large mercenary army to deal with such an invasion at that time. Serious invasion never came, however, and work at Colchester stopped at the second storey, where it remains today.

The White Tower, on the other hand, was finished in about 1097. Rather surprisingly, the Colchester and London keeps

Henry I's stone hall-keep of c. 1120 at Portchester, Hampshire, in a corner of the huge curtain-walled Roman brick fortress. The flat buttresses and two-light windows are typically Norman

were both supervised by Gundulf, Bishop of Rochester from 1077 until his death in 1108 – he had been appointed bishop by William's trusted Archbishop of Canterbury, Lanfranc, whose chamberlain he had been as a monk after the Conquest. The design produced by Gundulf and his masons was developed from recent keeps in Normandy and furnished a model for the many other hall-keeps in England: four storeys (in this and a few other cases each storey was split into more than one apartment), storerooms and a well below, two-storey hall above, and the lord or governor's private chamber or solar above that. In front of it there was originally a projecting forebuilding for the entrance; the surviving projection contains the chapel. The keep may have stood with only earthen and timber ramparts and the two sides of the Roman wall around its bailey, until Richard I added the inner stone curtain wall (including the partly surviving Bell Tower and Wardrobe Tower) right at the end of the Norman period in the 1190s, to form an inner ward.

Among the other Norman rectangular hall-keeps surviving in fair states of preservation are Henry I's at Portchester, Hampshire, of c. 1120 (in one corner of the titanic brick walls of the far larger 'Saxon Shore' fortress of late Roman times); Corfe Castle in Dorset (c. 1135); the Archbishop of Canterbury's at Rochester (a splendidly dramatic ruin, still with its forebuilding, built in c. 1130 with zigzag ornament appearing inside); Castle Hedingham, Essex (c. 1130); Norwich Castle (built by Hugh Bigod, the turbulent Norman magnate of East Anglia, in c. 1136); Castle Rising, Norfolk (c. 1138, by William de Albini, who married Henry I's widow); and Bamburgh Castle, Northumberland (which seems to have been built in c. 1140, during the chaotic reign of Stephen). All these great keeps have remains well worth visiting today – Bamburgh is still inhabited – though many Norman castles have later towers and outer walls that will be covered in the next volume of this series.

There followed a sequence of conventional hall-keeps built by that great ruler and restorer of order and civilisation, Henry II. Many of these were in the north, where the borders needed strengthening against the Scots: Scarborough, c. 1160, Appleby, c. 1160, Brougham, c. 1170, Richmond, c. 1170, Newcastle, c. 1170 and Carlisle, c. 1170. Henry destroyed many unlicensed castles built by barons during Stephen's reign, but he also licensed some himself: Geoffrey de Clinton's Kenilworth Keep, c. 1155 and Bishop Hugh Purset's at

The Archbishop of Canterbury's hall-keep of c. 1130 (still with its original entrance forebuilding) at Rochester, Kent

Norham, Northumberland, c. 1160, are good examples, and other more original designs will be mentioned later.

The barons and knights who took possession of England after the Conquest were culturally primitive except as soldiers. They were mentally equipped for slaughtering Saxon peasants if they gave any trouble, but not at all for the knightly pursuits and codes of behaviour that Romantic literature has imprinted on our minds. Such newly civilised ways emerged only during the middle 1100s, and the doors to those new ideas and others seem to have been opened by the Crusades.

The first Crusade was a confused reaction to the arrival of militant Islam in the Holy Land in 1095. The Duke of Normandy (Rufus's brother) and the Duke of Lorraine took

The round chapel (now roofless) of c. 1130 in Ludlow Castle, Shropshire. The doorway is little decorated, as was the early Norman tradition, but some zigzag ornament can be seen on the arches of the wall-seating arcades within

part in establishing the 'Latin Kingdom' in Jerusalem. The second Crusade came in 1147, during Stephen's troubled reign in England, when the Emperor of the Holy Roman Empire (largely Germany and Austria) and the King of France enabled the Latin Kingdom to survive a new threat, but failed to dislodge the Muslim control of the surrounding area. Western soldiers from all countries took part and brought back new ideas and tales of the advanced fortifications built by the Eastern Byzantine Empire and the Islamic forces. The third Crusade embarked in 1189 after Saladin of Damascus had taken Jerusalem and ended the Latin Kingdom (which had also secured Europe's trade route to the East). This time the kings of France and England (Richard I) as well as the emperor were involved, but despite some victories, the Crusade failed in its central purpose to save Jerusalem.

It was the first Crusade that initiated the Knights Hospitaller and Knights Templar in the 1120s, giving the world the image of the knight dedicated to guarding pilgrims and a sacred mission (and the round churches such as the chapel at Ludlow Castle in Shropshire of c. 1130, now roofless, derived from the Holy Sepulchre Church in Jerusalem). But it was the second Crusade that seems to have unleashed new types of castle design and an architectural flowering in the West, together with ideas of chivalry, idealised ladies, complex armour, violent and colourful tournaments and their slightly more controlled form, the 'Round Table' competitions.

In England Henry II's re-establishment of control by the monarchy from the time of his accession in 1154 was accompanied not only by the series of old-fashioned rectangular keeps already described, but by a number of experimental designs. The shortcoming of the rectangular keep was that its corners could not easily be defended from arrow-slits and were prone to undermining by tunnels, which were timber-supported until they were set on fire, after which the corner of the stone walls above would collapse. Round and polygonal plans, such as were reported from the Near East, would avoid that weakness. Henry II's engineer or 'ingeniator', Alnoth, produced at Orford in Suffolk the first of the polygonal designs in England – Henry had also built such a keep at Gisors in Normandy. The keep that Alnoth built at Orford in 1165–73, a direct assertion of royal authority over the obstreperous Bigod family that dominated East Anglia, survives almost intact but without its former curtain walls. The exterior has no less than eighteen sides plus a small

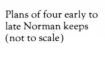

Plans of four early to
late Norman keeps
(not to scale)

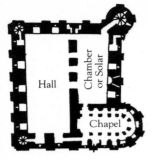

The White Tower, London
(c. 1078-97)

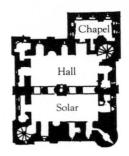

Rochester Castle, Kent (c. 1130)

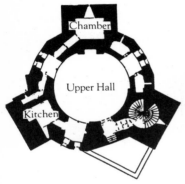

Orford Castle, Suffolk (1165-73)

Conisbrough Castle,
South Yorkshire (c. 1180)

entrance forebuilding between two of the three turrets that rise above the rest of the keep. The interior, however, is circular: the basement for storage and a well, the lower hall and the main hall occupying the second and third storeys, the chapel in the forebuilding's projection, and various dwelling rooms for the king's constable in the turrets (all still excellently preserved and restored). Polygonal experiments did not last long – Chilham in Kent and Odiham in Hampshire are the only other survivors, though some ruined shell-keeps such as Kilpeck in Hereford and Worcester also seem to have been multi-sided.

The experiment reached its logical conclusion with the circular keep, offering all-round vision for defenders and no corners to undermine. The first and most spectacular of these was one of those private castles that Henry II allowed only highly trusted nobles to build – in this case, his own half-brother Hameline Plantagenet, who had married the heiress of the Conqueror's great allies, the de Warenne family. In c. 1180 this couple built themselves Conisbrough Castle near Sheffield, which is both one of the most striking and the most attractive of Norman castles.

Conisbrough's visual impact is considerable, partly because of its position over the valley but more of the tremendous buttresses that run its entire height all around its circular central tower. These buttresses strengthen the keep (which has the finest ashlar stonework of any English castle) and contain the small chapel, garderobes and other chambers. The keep's attraction comes from the feeling that here at last is a castle for human beings to live in happily, not just a base from which to oppress the local inhabitants. It is quite small compared with the massive earlier hall-keeps. Despite its vanished floors, it is easy to imagine Hameline's feasts for his retainers in the main

Orford Castle, Suffolk. Henry II's polygonal keep was an experimental design of 1165–73 to overcome the vulnerability of square keeps which collapsed when their corners were undermined

Above: The first of the English round keeps: Conisbrough Castle, near Sheffield, South Yorkshire, built by Hameline Plantagenet, Henry II's half-brother, in c. 1180. The huge buttresses contain stairs, the chapel and other rooms

Left: A window, overlooking the bailey courtyard of Conisbrough Castle, in the private chamber of Plantagenet and his wife. The double window-seat in the thickness of the wall is a usual feature of the time

hall with its huge fireplace, his more intimate life with his lady in the chamber above (where there is a pretty little fireplace and a typically late Norman double seat in the splayed walls of the two-light window), and the popular tournaments in the inner ward below. This, one feels, represents the start of civilised life, at least for the ruling class.

After Conisbrough the round keep became the convention, but without the buttresses that could only leave angles prone to undermining. Other notable circular keeps include several along the Marches where the Welsh were causing increasing difficulties with their raids from the mountains, or along the good farmland of southern Wales which the Normans had occupied. They include those at Bronllys in Powys (1190s), Caldicot in Gwent (c. 1190), Dynevor in Dyfed (c. 1200), Skenfrith in Gwent (c. 1200) and Ewloe in Clwyd (after 1200, with a D-plan keep). Elsewhere there are fine round keeps at Barnard Castle in County Durham (c. 1190 by Bernard Baliol)

The fireplace in the round solar, or private chamber, on the level above the main hall of Conisbrough Castle

and Longtown in Hereford and Worcester (c. 1190). But perhaps the finest example of all is again in South Wales, at Pembroke Castle of c. 1200, far in the west. Here the great round keep has a magnificent stone vault inside and a large ward still enclosed by its lengthy and high Norman walls with square towers, though with many additional buildings of the following two centuries.

Henry II's last major castle was the largest of its time, high on the cliffs above Dover, guarding the English Channel more strongly than earlier Norman kings had felt necessary. Built in c. 1180–90, Dover Castle reverted to a huge rectangular keep, surrounded closely by the new-fashioned curtain walls with big rectangular wall-towers. He even started a second curtain outside the first, which was completed after 1200 by King John. The windows of Dover keep have mostly been altered now, but the finely zigzagged chapel is complete (with an unsuitable modern screen), the seemingly endless galleries, chambers and spiral stairs in the thickness of the wall can even now get a visitor lost, and in the basement the old archers' steps up to the arrow-slits can still be mounted. And, from a distance, the keep and its rings of walls form the most awe-inspiring sight.

If Dover is the grand finale of the Norman keep,

The unbuttressed round keep without any corners, a logical development from Orford and Conisbrough, and the extensive curtain walls of Pembroke Castle, Dyfed, South Wales, c. 1200. The original wall-towers were rectangular and their curving fronts are later additions

Framlingham in Suffolk – built by Roger Bigod in the 1190s after regaining the royal favour his father had lost – is prophetic of future castles. For here is another idea imported from the Crusades: one high curtain wall with no keep, but numerous large wall-towers around it, a pattern developed in the great castles of Edward I in the next century.

Outside England, the poorer barons of Scotland and Wales must have looked with envy at the stone walls of the Anglo-Norman border castles. It was only now, about 1200, that the earliest surviving stone castles by Welsh or Scottish masons were built. In northern Wales, near Betws-y-Coed, Dolwyddelan Castle was built in the 1190s and Llywelyn the Great was born there in 1200. The keep is small enough, even with the upper storey added later, but the site is memorable.

In Scotland there are just two stone castles of this period. Castle Roy, Highland Region, has a simple quadrangular curtain wall of c. 1200 around a courtyard in which there are some traces of living quarters. More impressive is the massively simple stone keep of the same date built by the Celtic-Norse chieftain of Knapdale, Sweyn, with flat

Towering above its harbour, Dover Castle, Kent, c.1170–80. Here, for the largest of all the Norman castles, Henry II's designer reverted to the old-fashioned massive rectangular hall-keep, but surrounded it with the new high curtain walls

Left: One of the first stone castles built by the Welsh, c. 1190 (the top was added later): Dolwyddelan Castle, on a steep hilltop in Gwynedd, North Wales, birthplace of Llywelyn the Great in 1200

Below: The start of a new era in castle design, with an idea imported from the East by returning Crusaders: Framlingham Castle, Suffolk, as built in c. 1190 by Roger Bigod, 2nd Earl of Norfolk. It has high curtain walls and square wall-towers, with no keep at all

The only surviving Scottish stone keep of the Norman period: Castle Sween, built by the Celtic-Norse lord of Knapdale in c. 1200 beside Loch Sween in Argyll, Strathclyde Region

buttresses of the Norman type and a big round-arched entrance, on the still remote shores of Loch Sween in Strathclyde Region. Nothing could demonstrate more vividly than the contrast between these simple stone forts and the complex designs of the English castles, the potency of the Normans' obsession with military power and efficiency expressed in massive stone.

Suggestions for Travellers

The best geographical group of Norman stone shell-keeps is the three in Devon and Cornwall. For hall-keeps, the northern border group in Cumbria, Northumberland and North Yorkshire is the most exciting, while those of the Welsh Marches from Shropshire down to Gwent are almost as evocative (the great northern Welsh castles were built after the Norman period), and those of Kent, Colchester and London the largest. East Anglia has some of the best experimental later keeps of Henry II's reign. But the maps and Gazetteer show that there are major Norman castle remains in many other counties, mostly with later additions.

3

NORMAN PARISH
AND SMALL
CHURCHES

Apart from the Romanesque splendours of the big abbeys and cathedrals, the keenest pleasures of Anglo-Norman architecture are to be found in exploring the parish churches of English villages and countryside – and lowland Scotland and Wales too. The maps and Gazetteer point out a selection of the best-preserved work of the Norman period, so giving travellers a start wherever they are in the country, but there are numerous other churches with worthwhile Norman features. For it seems that the basic distribution of parish churches in England (at least those built before the urban and suburban growth of Victorian times) was established in the late Anglo-Saxon and early Norman period. Later, as the population grew, the churches were rebuilt with larger spaces in whatever style was then the architectural fashion. Thus there are relatively few completely Norman churches; in many of the very finest quality, Gothic windows were later inserted to allow more light, aisles were often added with arcades of their own time to give more space for the congregation, chancels may have been entirely rebuilt in a different style, or the whole church may have been rescued from the ruined condition so common in the early 1800s, by Victorian restorers of varying sensitivity.

The state of the Church that the Normans imported to England was closely linked to the sources of its architecture. At the root were the Carolingian Empire's revival of western Christianity and its Romanesque art developed from the earliest Roman Christian forms. In Normandy Duke Richard II had persuaded St William, Abbot of Dijon, to bring the reform of the Benedictine monasteries to Fécamp, Jumièges and Bernay from 1002 onwards. From that time Norman architecture developed its own character, the most severely orderly and disciplined of all Romanesque regional varieties.

After the Conquest, there was an outburst of cathedral building in England, and an equivalent surge of parish church building on the estates of the new feudal landowners described in the last chapter. As they built their thousands of wooden castles, they swept away the Anglo-Saxon timber churches and replaced them in stone. These early Norman churches were usually tiny and not many have survived later enlarging. Perhaps the best place to get an idea of them is in a group in northern Surrey (Wisley, Pyrford and Farleigh), or another in the remote Wealden parts of northern Sussex (Selham, Stopham, Hardham and Buncton) where the simple plan of an unaisled nave and apsed chancel has been largely preserved through lack of later medieval population growth (these, as with other groups mentioned below, are marked on the relevant map). Another example, unique for having a timber frame and surviving, is the tiny single-space church at Winterborne Tomson, Dorset, while Moccas in Gloucester-

Early Norman architecture: Winterborne Tomson church, Dorset, one of the surviving small examples of before 1100. It has a single space of nave and semi-circular apse, of a kind widely built after the Conquest but usually enlarged later. Simple detail, here unusually of wood

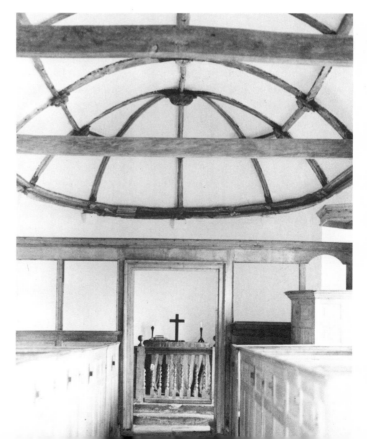

shire has the same simplicity on a larger scale. These little churches may date from somewhere between 1070 and 1100 – it is very rare for a Norman church to have a documented date, and the analysis of a church's decorative style, that can provide approximate dates for later Norman work, helps less in the case of such austerely unornamented buildings.

In other parts of the country there are many instances where it is hard to tell whether a church was built just before or after the Conquest. The churches were built at the expense of the new local lord and he employed what masons he could find, often local Anglo-Saxon craftsmen. Thus the charming little church of Winstone in Gloucestershire has what seems to be an Anglo-Saxon tower with a very early Norman apsed church. Similarly at Fingest in Buckinghamshire, the space under the Saxon-looking tower seems to have been used as the nave of the church (as in Anglian Barton-on-Humber), yet it probably dates from after the Conquest. Such churches have been dubbed the 'Saxon-Norman overlap' and walls of herringbone-pattern masonry are one of their commonest features.

Far more sophisticated architecture of c. 1080–90 – though still severely unornamented – can be seen on a small scale in St John's Chapel in the White Tower, Tower of London. Bishop Gundulf and his mason have made much of a limited area with a continuous apsed arcade and clerestory, with a barrel-vault above. The carving is limited to some scalloping and other early Norman motifs on the capitals. But the way that space is firmly contained by massive stone, yet made complex by its flow through the arcades, makes it a moving place to visit, for it is above all in the play of space with solid volumes that the greatness of Norman architecture lies.

Another example of this mastery of enclosed space is the parish church of St Nicholas, near the sea at Studland, Dorset – the nave and tower space here are of c. 1090–1100. An unaisled nave, a central tower, plus an apsed chancel are the next development from the very early unaisled nave-plus-apse plan. At Studland this can be seen scarcely altered – the exterior with its small round-headed windows, corbel-table (a row of carved heads running below the gutter), and flat buttresses of the typically Norman form against the tower (ready to support a higher tower than was ever built). And, inside, there is that fine series of spaces separated by big simply moulded round-headed arches, the chancel and rib-vaulting, probably added a little later (for rib-vaulting was evidently

A small early Norman church interior with more complex spaces: the chapel in the White Tower, Tower of London, c. 1078–97. It has a single space of nave and apse, but with an ambulatory and gallery around. The capitals are primitively carved

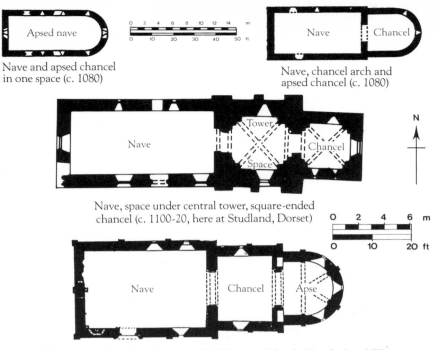

Nave and apsed chancel
in one space (c. 1080)

Nave, chancel arch and
apsed chancel (c. 1080)

Nave, space under central tower, square-ended
chancel (c. 1100-20, here at Studland, Dorset)

Nave, chancel and stilted apse (c. 1145, here at Kilpeck, Hereford and Worcester)

Norman parish church plans of increasing complexity (note two different scales)

Below left: An early Norman church exterior: Studland church, Dorset. The nave (on the right) is of the 1090s, the central tower and chancel a little later, still with their original small windows and corbel-table of carved faces under the eaves.

Below: The south doorway of Milborne Port church, on the borders of Somerset and Dorset, c. 1100–20. This is an early date for Norman figure carving in the capitals and the lions in the tympanum

developed in England at Durham, just before 1100).

Slightly later than Studland's nave is the grand Norman work at Milborne Port church, Somerset. The crossing arches and south doorway are strong forms of c. 1100–20, with fat undecorated roll-mouldings adding mass to the curve of each arch. By now the Normans had moved into the good farmland of South Wales and at St Clears church, Dyfed, the chancel arch is a charming and impressive climax to the long aisleless Norman nave, with two orders of plump roll-mouldings, the whole thing distorted by the centuries; one would date it c. 1110 in central England but the style may be later in outer Wales.

At Milborne Port the tympanum under the arch of the south door shows two dangerous-looking lions, rather well carved for the time, for the early Normans were abjectly bad at sculpture, though sometimes to the point where the work has the charm of children's art. Good instances of this include the tympana at Long Marton in Cumbria and Stoke-sub-Hamdon in Somerset, both seemingly of c. 1090–1100, with centaurs and dragons and a flying sword. Early fonts, such as those at St Martin's, Canterbury (locally and implausibly thought to be Saxon) and Kirkburn church in Humberside show a little more craftsmanship but their attraction is equally naïve.

The sort of tower that would have been built at Studland

Left: The chancel arch of St Clears church, Dyfed, South Wales, distorted by the weight above it. It is arch-stepped and roll-moulded, probably of c. 1120, with voluted and rather ornate scallop capitals

Right: Norman font of perhaps c. 1120 at Kirkburn church, Humberside, with crude but powerful figures, a monstrous winged serpent, intersecting arcade and interlace

The primitive tympanum over the north doorway of Stoke-sub-Hamdon church, Somerset. The relief sculpture shows a Tree of Life with birds, lamb cross, and the zodiac signs of Sagittarius and an unhappy Leo – all typical motifs of the years following 1100

may be seen in the massive west tower of Weaverthorpe church, Humberside, of c. 1110. In Scotland the old tradition of very tall towers on the east coast (as at pre-Norman Brechin) was continued with the round tower at Abernethy, Tayside, built at about the time the Normans took England. In 1072 William I invaded the south and east parts of Scotland, laid waste as far as the Tay river and the old Pictish capital, forced the Scottish King Malcolm Canmore to do homage to the English crown, and took his heir David back to 'Normanise' him in England. From then on the process of bringing at least the lowlands of eastern Scotland into the stream of European culture started. David I reigned from 1124 to 1153 and proved a great civilising king, for feudal order was a first step out of barbaric chaos, if a grim one. There is a fair number of Norman churches in these eastern parts of Scotland, as far north as the typical little aisleless nave-and-apse church at Birnie, Grampian Region, but the most interesting is St Rule's Church beside the ruins of the later St Andrews cathedral. It is recorded that St Rule's was built in 1140 (it may have been the

The west tower, c. 1110–20, of Weaverthorpe church, Humberside, with flat buttresses and early zigzag on the doorway arches

first cathedral there), but the soaring square tower that stood at its centre may well have gone up near the beginning of that century.

In England the end of the 1000s saw the most influential of all Anglo-Norman buildings in construction – the cathedral at Durham. Not only rib-vaulting was invented there, for zigzag or chevron ornament (the most typical form of Norman decorative stone carving) appeared at Durham first in c. 1110, intersecting blank arcading (another widespread favourite from 1110 onwards) before 1100, and the great carved drum-columns, adopted in a few other glorious churches, appeared first in the Durham nave. Rumours of the great cathedral must have spread soon after the transepts and nave were started in about 1110, and masons from all over England may have got their masters' permission to go and see it, for the Durham zigzag spread quickly. It is seen in an early primitive form at Goodmanham church in Humberside of 1120 or before (on the site where Edwin of Northumbria's pagan priest had desecrated his heathen temple and accepted Christianity 500 years earlier), and in countless other internal arches after that.

As for the Durham incised drum-piers, the job of making their precise geometric patterns fit from stone to stone of the columns seems to have proved too much for most masons of the 1120s and their appearances elsewhere are rare treasures. Among smaller churches there is a magnificent arcade at Pittington church in County Durham, with others in Kirkby Lonsdale church, Cumbria, and Compton Martin church in

St Rule's Church, St Andrews, Fife Region (with cathedral ruins in the background). St Rule's was probably the small first cathedral here and is usually dated c. 1140, but the tower is from an Anglo-Saxon tradition and may be considerably earlier

Somerset, as well as the shadowy eroded remains of yet another in the ruined part of Orford church, Suffolk. Most may date from c. 1120 or a little later, as do Durham-type arcades in major abbeys and cathedrals, which are described in Chapter 6.

Some Norman parish churches were built by the great monasteries themselves, if they stood on church land, but far the greater part was built by the local lords given land at the Conquest, or by their heirs. They built these stone churches to express thanks to God for their lands, for their own esteem with their church and lay peers, for their own salvation, and as a contribution towards the political stability of their properties. Traditionally, the gift of the priestly 'livings' for their churches also belonged to the local lord, though this caused regular disputes between Church and landowners when lords 'presented' their favoured priests to their bishops.

The standard of priests was not high, especially before 1150. They were little educated, often lax about such things as chastity, and lived poorly. Their living came from a tithe – a tenth of their congregations' crops, poultry, etc. – plus fees for baptism, marriages and funerals, any other offering by the local lord, and their own agricultural work. John of Ford's life of St Wulfric gives a taste of a priest's life in the 1130s. The

The nave arcade, of the 1120s, in Kirkby Lonsdale church, Cumbria, with alternating composite shafted and incised drum-piers of the type recently developed at Durham cathedral. The capitals are scalloped and, in the background, voluted

priest at Haselbury, Somerset (where Wulfric was a hermit) was called Brictric. He had a wife, and a son who later followed him as parish priest. Brictric spent almost the whole of his days and nights chanting psalms and praying in the church, for constant adoration of God was very much the primary function of all medieval priests and churches. He would ride home on his horse (itself a luxury) for meals and then, unless he had work to do on his strip of land, return to the church for more worship. His son Osbern did not marry, and when he became priest he slept in the church. Another priest from a nearby parish is mentioned too; he had four sons, all of whom entered the monastery at Ford Abbey. By 1150, such priests were visited every year by the bishop's archdeacon or rural dean to check that the standard of worship was maintained.

By the 1130s radical changes in parish church building were under way. These affected both the plan and architectural details. The most noticeable changes in the plans were that the typical apse imported from France disappeared and chancels were built square-ended, while after 1150 arcaded aisles and west towers became increasingly frequent. The square-ended chancel had been a late Anglo-Saxon tradition and the disappearance of the apse (in cathedrals as well as churches) has been interpreted as a triumph of the native custom in England, though some early Norman churches have square chancels too. On balance, it seems more likely that the prime cause was a change in ritual, calling for larger east windows to let in the morning sunlight – for apses impose small windows. Yet even that is not a fully satisfying explanation, as some square-ended chancels were built with no east window at all in the West Country. Whatever the reason, so many chancels were rebuilt square-ended that the spatial beauty of the surviving apses is invested with special value.

It was also in about 1130 that the marvellous period of English Romanesque decorative carving began, perhaps instigated by the spread of continental craftsmanship from the Cluniac monastery at Lewes. Sir Alfred Clapham's classic *English Romanesque Architecture* points out that just about every ornamental feature used in late Anglo-Norman architecture until the period ends around 1200, was introduced between 1130 and 1150. For dating this work, Clapham evolved a system, refined by later scholars, of identifying the earliest likely date for most features that are found in Norman churches up and down the land, though subject to some local quirks. An account of the chief of these will be helpful to travellers using this guide, together with the developments of architectural features up to 1130 already described. Most of the features mentioned are illustrated in the photographs and named in the captions.

1130 ONWARDS. The *zigzagged chevron* motif becomes increasingly popular, often appearing in several neighbouring bands and in enriched complex forms. Ornately *sculpted capitals* become more common. *Volute capitals* become rarer, though they and *scalloped capitals* (the number of scallops increasing later) appear throughout the period. *Disc* patterns, often arranged like *fish-scales*, become popular, especially in East Anglia. Ornament consisting of motifs such as the *billet* (like small sections of a round rod), *reel* (like narrow-waisted cotton reels, so roughly forming an H shape in profile) and *pellet* (like simple projecting beads) in lines, often with the

Right: The Herefordshire master-carver's famous south doorway of c. 1145 at Kilpeck church. Monsters and interlaced trails run up the responds and reveals, and there is zigzag and a flowering plant with pellet motif in the tympanum. The arch is of four orders; the innermost is roll-moulded, and the others have projecting zigzag, elaborated beakhead, etc., with more monsters and zodiac creatures in linked compartments (like developed rosettes) around the hood

Left: A richly carved late Norman church interior: Stewkley church, Buckinghamshire (c. 1140–50), showing the scalloped capitals with beakhead and zigzag orders on the windows, tower space and chancel arches. The square-ended chancel is more typical of late Norman plans than Kilpeck's rounded apse

reel and billet alternating, appears increasingly in combination with bands of other motifs. Standards of *tympanum* carving are still irregular, but some show improved craftsmanship. Intersected blank *arcading* (the arches overlapping each other), already a popular decorative feature, sometimes appears with zigzag arches.

1140 ONWARDS. *Zigzag* becomes increasingly complex, sometimes taking on squared forms like battlements (Lincoln cathedral west front) or in two rows forming a *lozenge* pattern (Stoke-sub-Hamdon church, Somerset). *Foliage* carving is now increasingly rich, with figures sometimes among the tendrils, and taking on a slightly Celtic flavour in the Shobdon and Kilpeck 'school' of Herefordshire. Doorways and arches of several ornate orders (side-shafts and arch-bands) become increasingly widespread, employing motifs such as *beakhead* (birds' faces looking straight out and seeming to grip the stone moulding with their beaks), *cable* (like a rope), *rosettes* (flat circles, with concentric or other carving in each), and *diaper*

The south doorway, Newbald church, Humberside (c. 1140–50), of four orders, with inventive voluted, etc., capitals, arch with zigzag, roll-moulding and cable-pattern. Above, there is a seated Christ in a part-*vesica* niche with interlace and zigzag surround, and higher still, a corbel-table of faces (plain checkers, diagonal squares, sometimes with interlace work). *Tympanum* and other figure carving improves.

1150 ONWARDS. *Figure sculpture* improves further, partly through the introduction of the southern French sculpture revival by the Cluniacs via Lewes Abbey, East Sussex, and their new foundation at Reading, c. 1130. *Sculpted capitals* become commoner. *Sculpted multi-order doorways* become the norm. *Beakhead* decoration has animal faces almost as often as birds.

1160 ONWARDS. *Zigzag* ornament now sometimes projects from a wall or arch, as well as lying along it, producing a new three-dimensional encrusted look. Many of the most richly ornamented multi-order archways date from this time onwards. At the same time, some forms introduced by the Cistercian monks' less ornamented architecture start to appear, though these are scarcely seen outside their monasteries before 1170: the *corbel* (projecting from a wall to support the springer of a vault); the *waterleaf capital* (with various simple leaves, rather than the earlier motifs carved on capitals) and its accompanying *bell capital* (as against the old basically cuboid cushion capital); together with *pointed arches*. The *abacus* (the stone between the capital of a pier and the arch above it) is occasionally made polygonal or round, as against the invariable rectangular shape of earlier abaci.

1170 ONWARDS. *Complex enriched intersecting arcading* appears (as on the porch of Bishop's Cleeve church, Gloucestershire). *Porches*, very rare earlier, are now occasionally built. *Pointed arches* start to appear above a few Norman piers. The carved bands of multi-ordered doorways, usually firmly compartmented earlier, start to flow with less interruption.

1180 ONWARDS. *Zigzag* occasionally develops into *key-pattern* or *chain-pattern* (Barfreston church and St David's cathedral). *Rosettes* develop into carved *medallions* on the bands of multi-order doorways (Lady Chapel at Glastonbury). Zigzag and other *transverse moulding* appears on the underside of arches at times (Steyning church, West Sussex). Standards of *figure sculpture* are further improved. Most of the earliest surviving English *stained glass* (Canterbury and York), *paving* (Byland Abbey, North Yorkshire) and *wall paintings* (in several Sussex churches, Copford church in Essex, and Barfreston church in

The west front of
Iffley church, Oxford
(c. 1170), a complete
late Norman church,
showing multiple
zigzag and beakhead
ornament, and spiral
shafts on the upper
windows (circular
window added later)

Kent, *et al.*) are of this decade or a little earlier, though some paintings (at Hardham church, West Sussex, for example) have been dated as far back as c. 1130.

From this later Norman period hundreds of richly carved doorways, chancel arches, corbel-tables, arcades and windows survive, often added to simple earlier churches, but sometimes done as an integrated part of a newly-built church. Such complete examples of the time, their fizzing zigzag and other carved ornament heightening the resonant series of spaces within, may be found at Stewkley, Buckinghamshire (c. 1140–50), Kilpeck, Hereford and Worcester (c. 1145–50), Newbald, Humberside (c. 1150, though with some later alterations), Iffley, just outside Oxford (c. 1170), and at other villages around England. But parts added to several churches throughout the country – such as the almost Gothic chancel of New Shoreham church in West Sussex (c. 1180) or the work at East Meon, Hampshire – can also give the visitor pleasure.

In Scotland the Norman-educated King David I was doubtless influential in the appearance of a crop of excellent Norman churches in Lothian and across the Firth of Forth, several of which can still be seen. In addition, there are memorable little Norman chapels at Edinburgh Castle and St Oran's beside Iona cathedral. The finest of all Norman churches in Scotland are at Dalmeny in Lothian (c. 1150) and Leuchars in Fife, dated at c. 1195 though in parts looking earlier – the contrast between the richly arcaded exterior and the internal severity is extraordinary.

One ruin of a small church on a Scottish island, Mainland Orkney, is of a rare type associated with the Knights Templar. The round church at Orphir is now only a fragment, but other churches with the circular plan of the church of the Holy Sepulchre in Jerusalem (brought to the West by the Knights Templar) do survive from the Norman period. These are the chapel at Ludlow Castle, Shropshire (c. 1120, now roofless), St Sepulchre at Northampton, St Sepulchre at Cambridge (both of c. 1130), and the Temple Church of c. 1160–80, south of Fleet Street in London (which combines Norman characteristics and pointed arches).

In Wales there are two lovely abbey churches (Penmon and Ewenny) that are described in Chapter 6, and a few minor parish churches. Of these, Kerry church in Powys has an

The late Norman style: an ambitious parish church of the 1140s, seen from the east – the apse and (beyond) chancel, nave and belfry of Kilpeck church, Hereford and Worcester (c. 1145–50). This church is one of the primary examples, inside and out, of the newly accomplished architectural carving of the so-called Shobdon school. The corbel-table of carved heads, seen here on the apse, continues around the church, and the belfry is also sculpted

arcade of c. 1175 interesting for its primitive severity, while the delicious little Llanrhwydrys church on Anglesey has Norman features and a cruck-framed structure of indeterminable date. Finally, one monument must be mentioned, for it is well worth the trek up the remote valley in Powys to Pennant Melangell. Here, in an outhouse of the church, St Melangell's elegant shrine of c. 1160 has been carefully reconstructed from fragments found where this royal patron saint of the hares found refuge from her Irish suitors in the Dark Ages.

Late Norman carved decoration in Scotland at Leuchars church, Fife Region (c. 1195), showing blind and intersecting arcading, with zigzag and cable-pattern enrichment of chancel and apse, and a corbel-table above

Suggestions for Travellers

In England it is hard to find a county that has no churches with work of good quality from the late flowering of the Anglo-Norman Romanesque in 1140–1200, but some particularly rich areas can be pointed out: Kent, east of Canterbury (Barfreston above all); the broad coastal strip of West Sussex (especially the two Shoreham churches); eastern Hampshire; the Cotswold borders of Gloucestershire and Wiltshire (combining earlier and late Norman, as at Elkstone); the extraordinary area around Hereford (notably Kilpeck and Shobdon) and Gloucester; southern Oxfordshire and western Berkshire; parts of Cambridgeshire and inland Suffolk; northern Warwickshire; southern Shropshire; the area east of Sheffield; and the villages north of York. There is a series of varied Norman churches in what is now northern Humberside – to start at Weaverthorpe in the north and drive southwards visiting the five churches ending at Newbald makes a memorable day. But there are many others to be discovered too – the areas suggested here do not cover such intact Norman church masterpieces as Stewkley, Buckinghamshire, and Iffley, outside Oxford.

St Melangell's restored shrine, c. 1160, at Pennant Melangell, Powys, Wales. This is the burial place of the Irish princess who became the patron saint of hares

4

NORMAN HOUSES – COUNTRY AND TOWN

To get a glimpse of people's lives at the time when the few Norman houses surviving today were built, and to imagine the houses themselves in their contemporary setting, one needs a picture of the English countryside and towns during the 1100s. In south-eastern England most of the country was cleared and being farmed by thousands of small village communities, though a traveller would have seen more woodland among the fields than he does today. The Weald, stretching through central Kent and into northern Sussex, remained more densely wooded. Moving outwards from the south-east, great stretches of Hampshire (New Forest), Hertfordshire (Epping), Berkshire (Windsor Forest), the band between Oxford and Stamford, Hereford and Worcester, Lincolnshire, Nottinghamshire (Sherwood), Derbyshire (High Peak) and Lancashire (Lonsdale) were reserved as the King's Forest. All these royal forests protected wild boar and the three native kinds of deer. Such sources of meat were of course much poached, but the law of the land did not run here and Norman kings ordained the harshest penalties in an effort to preserve their favourite sport. They did, however, sell 'warrening rights' to encourage local people to kill wild cat, fox, badger and wolf in the forests.

Further north there were more King's Forests in Yorkshire, Northumberland and Cumbria, but there were few people living here after William I's slaughterous devastation of 1070, in reprisal for their bid for freedom, until the Cistercian monks resettled the area in the 1150s. In Scotland and Wales by that time, the Norman feudal system extended throughout the good lowland farmland, leaving mountainous and remote areas to their old ways. At Birsay (Orkney), Freswick

(Caithness) and Jarlshof (Shetland) there are extensive remains of Scottish-Norse villages still ruled by their own lords in the 1100s – they lived in timber and turf Long Houses of the reasonably snug sort like the undatable Black Houses of the Outer and some Inner Hebrides (Tiree, notably), still inhabited today.

In Normanised England the kings adopted the efficient Anglo-Saxon administrative and tax machinery, as well as many of the Saxon laws. The old system of shires and hundreds, sheriffs and other royal agents, was merged easily enough with the feudal barons' new powers and the Church's rights, but Latin replaced English as the language of government processes and of literature. In the villages a countrywide system was developed (with some variations, especially in the old Danelaw). Each village had two, or rarely three, immense open fields of at least 100 acres – an Anglo-Saxon tradition. These were divided into strips – some allotted to the local lord, one to the priest, the rest to individual villagers – and all the village shared the communal parts of the work in the big field being cultivated that year, ploughing, sowing and harvesting. Pigs and cows were kept on the common grazing land in summer but were difficult to feed in winter. Most men and women were tied to their village life by the feudal laws and to them travel was unknown.

Little is known of the long-vanished village houses of the time, for they have been built over repeatedly. Most were of timber, with local building materials such as thatch, wattle, clay and turf used in various ways. In western England, cruck-frames of timber – giant curving beams providing the outline of both walls and gabled roof – were probably in use by the 1100s, though none of the survivors has been carbon-dated quite as far back.

So most villages of 1100 were groups of little wood or wattle and clay houses with plots for poultry, clustered around a small stone church. Later in that century, stone was used in wealthier village houses and two of these survive in part. In the remote village of Blisland on the edge of Bodmin Moor in Cornwall, the seventeenth-century manor-house facing the village green has a wing on one flank with a doorway and two tiny windows set in massive masonry. The round-headed arches are cut from single stones, which would be a sign of pre-Norman work in central England but might well date from the early 1100s in this Celtic province.

The other village house is of more sophisticated work dating from c. 1150. This is the little stone house tucked behind a shop building in the High Street of West Malling, Kent, with a zigzagged round-topped Norman window. It has been called a Prebendary House, linking it to nearby Malling Abbey, but it may equally well have been connected with the local castle (also surviving in part).

By 1150 the countryside was settled enough for some local lords to move out of their timber castles and into stone manor-houses. The earliest survivors are probably Saltford Manor (Avon), Hemingford Grey Manor (Cambridgeshire) and the ruined Portslade Manor (East Sussex), all of c. 1150. Saltford Manor, with its tall proportions, splendid zigzagged two-light window and internal simple round-arched doors, is an excellent representative (despite its many alterations) of what was probably a widespread type. The hall would have been on the upper floor behind the fine window, with the solar or private chamber at the other end, and storage and work space below. At Hemingford Grey, it is the impressive hall itself that survives. Other evocative country manors, of only a little later, are Burton Agnes Old Manor (Humberside) and Charleston Manor (East Sussex), both dated c. 1170–80 by Margaret Wood, the leading authority on medieval houses.

The late Norman manor-house: Saltford Manor, near Keynsham, Avon (c. 1150). The tall proportions, small windows and two-light round-arched window (with zigzag and other decoration) are typical of the manor-houses (with upper-floor hall and solar, or private chamber) which some local lords preferred to their fathers' small timber castles by this time. The out-house, two windows and buttresses are post-Norman

All the houses mentioned so far are still lived in privately and unexpected visitors are quite reasonably unwelcome. But the two best examples of late Norman country houses are open to visitors. One of these is the apogee of the small manors already mentioned, Boothby Pagnell Manor, Lincolnshire, of c. 1190–1200, standing unused in the grounds of the Regency house called Boothby Pagnell Hall, just outside the little village with its Norman church.

Here, at Boothby Pagnell, one gets a clear impression of life in such local landowners' houses. From the outside, the rugged arches of the lower storey reflect its use for labour and storage; inside, the spaces have plain stone walls with a splendid rib-vaulted undercroft over the room on the left, and a tunnel-vault on the right. Outside again, the entrance to the first-floor living hall is up an external stone stairway on the left to a round-arched doorway, while the original Norman two-light window of the private room, the solar, can be seen on the right (the large window to the hall is of the 1400s, when the Norman stone window was moved around the corner to the left). A modern slate roof replaces the original thatching. Inside, the main hall is remarkably complete, with its great stone-hooded fireplace resting on corbels (which dates it to late in the 1100s), beamed ceiling, triangular-headed aumbry in the wall, and simply arched stone doorway into the solar. The mind can drape the walls with hangings, cover the floor with straw or rushes, furnish the space with strong oak furniture, and people it with the local lord's family about their work and pleasures. And in the solar, the usual Norman double seat, in the thickness of the wall beside the window, conjures up the quieter moments of the owner and his wife.

On a grander scale still were the Halls of the great barons and bishops. From the early Norman period there survive in ruins the Hall of Richmond Castle (North Yorkshire), from c. 1160 that of Christchurch Castle and from c. 1190 the undercroft of Eynsford (Kent); and the whole Hall of Oakham Castle (Leicestershire) survives. There are ruins of bishops' palaces at Winchester and Bishops Waltham, Hampshire, while the great Hall of Bishop Auckland palace is now its chapel. Oakham is especially well-preserved and evocative, for it is all that survives of the castle and that seems to symbolise the move towards civilised houses. The Hall is on a large scale, with a stone wall and timbered roof, and two tall arcades of circular piers and round-topped arches dividing it into nave and aisles. The stone carving is of fine quality, in a style that Sir

Left: Boothby Pagnell Manor, Boothby Pagnell, Lincolnshire (c. 1190–1200). This classic late Norman manor-house has rustic doors and windows for the ground-floor working and storage rooms, and a more accomplished round-arched doorway and two-light window (the big window is a late medieval alteration) for the living hall and solar (private chamber) on the upper level, approached by an external stone stairway

Right: Living hall, Boothby Pagnell, with a late Norman corbelled fireplace, beamed ceiling and a round-arched window now blocked

Below left: Triangular-headed aumbry or cupboard at Boothby Pagnell, and a round-arched doorway from the hall into the solar, with the solar's double-seat window, in the thickness of the wall, visible beyond

Right: Plan of Boothby Pagnell Manor

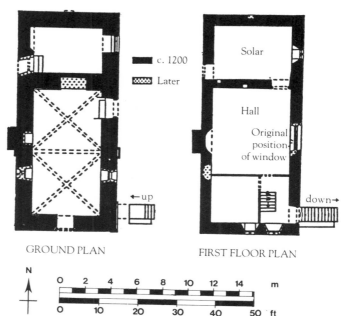

GROUND PLAN   FIRST FLOOR PLAN

Nikolaus Pevsner has linked with the Canterbury masons of a little earlier than its date of c. 1190.

The towns of any size in England of the 1100s were few, and even those would seem tiny by today's standards. London, with a population of some 18,000 (but growing quickly throughout the century) was by far the largest, then came York with about 8,000 people, Lincoln with 6,000, and others with 3,000 or less – Ipswich, Norwich, Southampton, Bristol, Cambridge and Huntingdon. Winchester had 6,000 people at the time of the Domesday Book (1086) but declined to 1,500

The stone Merchant's House of c. 1150, embedded in a later medieval stretch of Southampton town walls, formerly opening on to the town quay. The round-arched doorway and slit window led into the storerooms; the two-light window above marks the merchant's dwelling quarters

by the year 1200. Of these towns there are few domestic remains, but one can imagine timber and clay houses in narrow streets recorded as prone to frequent and devastating fires. Only in the 1190s did the mayor of London make the first regulations requiring stone walls for new houses – brick-making had not yet been re-invented.

Southampton was already important as a port, trading with Scandinavia, the Low Countries and, increasingly after the Conquest, with France. The town was walled in late Norman times and a stretch of that wall survives (between later medieval stretches) below the site of the now-vanished castle keep. Further along the walls to the right is a preserved section of the medieval town. Among its narrow streets are the walls of two Norman town houses. The Merchant's House of c. 1150 is partly embedded into the later town wall. The walls of the house survive intact with the ground-floor doorway that gave ready access from its storeroom on to the main quay beyond the town walls, and the round-arched two-light windows of the living quarters above. Further along the town wall, in Porter Lane, is the Long House of c. 1180 (often misleadingly called Canute's Palace). It has a long thin plan and enough survives of its ruined walls and Norman windows to show that here again the living rooms were upstairs.

No Norman houses remain in London, but town houses of the time – altered to varying degrees – can be seen at Norwich (the 'Music House', of c. 1175), Cambridge (the 'School of

Town walls: one of the rare stretches of pre-1200 town walls to survive is this section, below the site of the demolished castle, at Southampton, Hampshire. The flat unstepped buttresses are typically late Norman

Pythagoras', of c. 1200) and Bury St Edmunds (Moyses Hall, of c. 1180). There are other fragments too, such as the interior wall and window of c. 1200 behind No. 52A Stonegate in York, and the extraordinary doorway in the main street of Milborne Port, Somerset. But Lincoln is unique in having three well-preserved town houses of the period. Walking from the Norman west front of Lincoln cathedral out of the precinct gate, and turning left down Steep Hill, one soon comes to the Norman House of c. 1170–80 with a reconstructed two-light window on the left (at one time it was incorrectly called Aaron's House). Further down, Steep Hill becomes The Strait and here on the right stands the famous Jew's House. This splendid residence for the time is also of c. 1170–80, its

Left: The extraordinary doorway, probably of c. 1200, of a house in the main street of Milborne Port, Somerset. The ornate segmental arch has zigzag on the jambs

Right: The Norman House, Steep Hill, Lincoln (c. 1170–80), with its eroded hood-moulded (on figure-sculpted corbels) doorway, and restored two-light window of the dwelling quarters above

storeroom ground floor now opened up into shop-fronts, but still with its hooded doorway, chimney-breast and two round-arched windows to the upper living quarters (presumably the roof would have been of thatch). These houses were almost certainly of stone because they sheltered the coinage and documents of the wealthy Jewish bankers who financed armies and building projects for Norman kings, barons and bishops at a time when Christians were banned from lending on interest. Aaron of Lincoln was the most eminent of these, though Jacob of Canterbury (whose undercroft can still be seen under the County Hotel there) ran him a close second.

The Strait in Lincoln becomes the very long High Street at the bottom of the hill and this, passing three Anglo-Saxon church towers on the way, finally reaches on the left the large house of c. 1180–90 called St Mary's Guild. This area was the most fashionable suburb at the time and the mayor of Lincoln lived next door. It seems that the house – whose interiors and walls, complete with windows and grand courtyard entrance arch, are still there – was the residential headquarters of a guild combining piety with crafts and trade.

For twelfth-century English people effectively combined business with religion, and the Church too made sure of its share of the proceeds to support its great settlements. At Glastonbury, the monks dug up what they claimed to be the

Above: The Jew's House, The Strait, Lincoln (c. 1170–80). It has an ornately carved hood-moulded doorway under the upper floor's chimney-breast, and two round-arched two-light windows to the living rooms above, with typical Norman string-courses

Right: Interior of the single-aisled hall of Eastbridge Hospital, St Peter's Street, Canterbury (c. 1180–90), with Transitional pointed arches with chamfered step and a fine Romanesque wall-painting of Christ in a *vesica pisces*

St Mary's Guild House, High Street, Lincoln (c. 1180–90), with complex archway, flat buttresses, late Norman windows and carved string-course

bodies of Arthur and Guinevere, and made their tomb an extra goal for pilgrims. At Canterbury, a new saint was added to St Augustine when Thomas à Becket was martyred in 1170, and the pilgrims there multiplied. As the city prospered, living accommodation was built for wealthy pilgrims and then, as an act of piety out of the proceeds, for the infirm or impoverished

aged of the town. Such an institution can still be seen in the interior of the Eastbridge Hospital, built in c. 1180–90 in St Peter's Street, Canterbury. It has a vaulted crypt on its ground floor, while above is a chapel and a lofty single-aisled hall, whose serene Romanesque wall-painting and pointed Transitional arches signal the building as a stepping-stone between the Norman age and the Gothic architecture that followed.

Suggestions for Travellers

The Norman houses at Southampton, the fragment at York and Boothby Pagnell (ask at the main house nearby) are open to visitors, while the Jew's House and Norman House in Lincoln are shops. The 'Music House' at Norwich, Moyses Hall at Bury St Edmunds, and the Eastbridge Hospital at Canterbury are museums which have normal daytime opening. The ruins of the bishop's palace at Bishops Waltham and the various castle Halls can also be visited normally. But the other houses are private and those wishing to see the interiors should write well ahead of their visit to the proprietor for permission.

5

NORMAN MONASTERIES

The Normans arrived in England at a time when they themselves were experiencing a revival and purging of
monastic life. They brought their own senior clergy and the
Church was given a quarter of all English land by William I. So
at once the monasteries became one of the chief influences in
the daily life of many ordinary people. The Norman
foundations sprang up all over the kingdom and grew
throughout the following centuries. Surprisingly, little can be
seen today – the abbey or priory churches described in the next
chapter are the most frequent survivors, for they were often
bought by their local citizens to act as parish churches after
Henry VIII dissolved the monasteries themselves in the 1530s.
But there was no such continuing use for most of the cloisters,
refectories, chapter houses and dormitories around them –
these were usually burned or soon fell into ruin, their stones
taken for other buildings. To understand the ruins, it will be
most useful to concentrate in this chapter on one outstanding
site of each of the major orders.

Monasticism was in decline in Britain in the 1060s, for the
shattering campaigns of the second Danish invasions – led by
Sweyn Forkbeard around 1000 and leading to his son Cnut
becoming king of all England – had destroyed almost all the
pious settlements built up so recently by St Dunstan. Nor did
the movement recover before William I's conquest – there
were a mere thirty small Benedictine monasteries scattered
around southern England, and just two in the north. Only in
such remote places as Orkney, where the Deerness monks
were presumably Norse, and Llantwit Major in South
Glamorgan, may other small foundations have survived. The
Norman Benedictine monks were swift to take over the

decayed Anglo-Saxon houses and to found new ones, even in the north of England and south-west Wales. William made ferocious expeditions to these parts from 1069 onwards and encouraged the establishment of monasteries at St David's and Durham, to venerate the relics of David and of Cuthbert, probably taking the view that they would do just as much to keep order as his castles could. William himself founded one monastery, at Battle in East Sussex, where he had defeated Harold.

After the king's destruction of northern England, a monk called Aldwine rescued the revered buildings at Jarrow in 1074, revived the monastery of Bede and built the upper part of the central tower (perhaps the earliest Norman monastic work still to be seen) before the monks were drawn in to the great regional magnet of Durham in 1083. Monasteries were re-established at York and Whitby at about the same time.

Benedictine monasticism, which the Normans encouraged in its reformed version, was the original monastic 'rule' of the Church. The order had been founded by St Benedict at his monastery of Monte Cassino, north of Naples, in the early 500s. It was then just one of many monasteries, but Benedict's rule – not too harsh, but requiring obedience, poverty, regular prayer, manual work and scholarship – was taken by the Church for its wider model from 650 onwards. The Benedictine order (known as the Black Monks, from their clothing) spread widely in France in the 800s and reached England in about 950. Its monasteries in France were becoming lax by then, which led to the first reform movement started by some monks who founded the famous Abbey of Cluny in 910. The Cluniac reforms affected most Benedictine houses, from within their own order, by the time of the conquest of England. And in about 1090 the Cluniac Benedictines themselves started work on the Abbey of Lewes, in East Sussex, colonised direct from Cluny and copying the French church's amazing east end with five radiating apsed chapels. The great buildings at Cluny and Lewes are no more than shadowy fragments now, but the seeds of the Cluniac ideal of fine architecture and rich carving, as a glorification of God, found fertile soil in England after 1120. Much Wenlock, Thetford, Monkton Farleigh and Reading were slightly later Cluniac monasteries, and at Castle Acre (Norfolk) much of the splendour of their ornate architecture can still be seen.

The majority of early Norman monasteries in England, however, were mainsteam Benedictine. That included the greater part of the bishops' cathedrals, for those at Canterbury, Norwich, Rochester, Durham, Ely, Winchester, Worcester and others were staffed by the monks of the Benedictine monasteries built beside them (the rest of the cathedrals were staffed by canons, who were ordained priests, as we shall see later). There were other Benedictine monasteries too, great abbeys such as at St Albans, headed by an abbot, and the lesser priories headed by a prior or prioress. The major Norman nunneries have been destroyed to an even greater extent than the monasteries – their greatest monument is the abbey church at Romsey, Hampshire, but none of their domestic buildings remains there.

Many of these Benedictine cathedrals and major abbey churches have scraps of old monastic buildings scattered near them, but only two have considerable remains. At Norwich, although the cloister-walks themselves were rebuilt after 1200, much of the Norman infirmary, parlatorium (now the Song School), tunnel-vaulted Dark Entry passage and part of the refectory can still be seen around the cloister.

The best Benedictine remains of all are at Canterbury (beside the cathedral, not at St Augustine's ruined abbey on St Martin's Hill). Here one can get a real feeling of the grandeur of the monks' domestic surroundings, of the monastery's growth from its start, and of the changing Norman styles. The brethren's chief function was to maintain the *Opus Dei* (God's work), the regular round of services worshipping the Creator in the archbishop's great cathedral. So the monastic buildings nestle against the cathedral walls, here on the north side of the church rather than the customary south. The Norman main cloister, with its flanking chapter house and refectory, was rebuilt later in Gothic style. But the rest of the major buildings erected between about 1090 and 1160 can be traced, many of them still intact, among the houses and other changes of the subsequent eight centuries.

First of all in date there is the immense undercroft beneath the spacious upper-level monks' dormitory, started under Archbishop Lanfranc in the late 1080s and still being built (judging by the appearance of some early zigzag) in about 1110. The undercroft is not easily viewable, but over its north-east corner, part of the dormitory itself can be seen. East of the dormitory lie the two surviving walks of the so-called Infirmary Cloister and, beyond that, there runs a length of one lofty arcaded wall – all that survives of the inexplicably huge infirmary built in c. 1120 with simple early Norman detailing.

Looking through the arches of the infirmary wall, buildings of the next two stages can be seen – the exterior of Archbishop Anselm's Chapel (with restrained decoration that looks to be of c. 1120–30, though Anselm died in 1109) and, next to it, the gorgeous treasury with the rich architectural forms and abstract carved ornament of c. 1150, full of inventive motifs.

Returning to the two-sided Infirmary Cloister (one arcaded side is of c. 1150, the other of nearer 1190), the next particular pleasure is the marvellously vaulted round undercroft of the Lavatorium (washing room) Tower, supported by ingenious rib-vaults (with roll-moulding and billet pattern) that spring from twin central piers and are surrounded by a zigzagged arcade forming three-quarters of a circle. The tower above has gone, but this little *tour-de-force* is clearly again of c. 1150.

The final group of Norman monastic buildings at Canterbury lies 200 yards away in the far corner of Green Court, the lawned garden facing the open side of the Infirmary Cloister. It consists of the Court Gatehouse, the North Hall

Benedictine monastery architecture: the treasury of c. 1150, beside the east end of Canterbury cathedral. It has rich late Norman carving, with zigzagged arches to the undercroft, other ornate carving on the windows, string-courses and blank arcading of the main storey above

The passage from the crypt to the Infirmary Cloister, with the circular rib-vaulted undercroft of the Benedictine monks' Lavatorium (wash-room) Tower (c. 1150), Canterbury cathedral monastery

and its grand staircase, all added at the public entrance side of the monastic precinct in about 1160–70. The North Hall is typical of other living halls of the time (see Chapter 4) in being on the upper floor (the interior was rebuilt in 1843 in Norman style), with an undercroft below. Both here and in the gatehouse there is a new, almost urbane, serenity in the design of the frontages – compare these relaxed proportions with the fierce decorative intensity of the treasury, for example. But it is the stairway that draws the eye. The roof is a happy enough Victorian design, while the tremendous lower piers, the slender shafts up the sloping sides and the vividly enriched arches are of c. 1160, forming a small masterpiece.

Although no other English Benedictine monastery has Norman work on the scale of Canterbury, some notable works of architecture remain elsewhere. There are extensive remains, though mostly of a later date, at Dunfermline Abbey in Scotland. At Worcester cathedral the Benedictine monks in about 1120 produced the first chapter house with a round plan, the roof supported by a central pier with radiating vaults. And another major Benedictine work is the masterful Norman gatehouse, the only surviving twelfth-century piece of the destroyed great abbey, at Bury St Edmunds, Suffolk. The gatehouse was completed in 1148 and it combines a general early Norman military feeling with an outburst of delicate

abstract ornament in its carved detail. The entrance arch, projecting like a porch, has billet, fish-scale and cable motifs, while higher up there are intersecting arcades and arches with several novel motifs – all tightly held as a composition by the plain corner buttresses.

The other important religious order of early Norman times in England was the Augustinian Canons. They were not monks, but ordained priests living communally and, like Benedictine monks, devoted to the *Opus Dei* of their cathedral. Yet the order of Augustinian Canons (later known as Austin Canons) also founded its own abbey settlements away from the cathedrals, living what were in effect monastic lives to the rule that St Augustine of Hippo (not to be confused with our Augustine of Canterbury) had composed for his saintly sister in the fifth century. Augustine had in his writing projected a powerful image of the Christianised earth becoming the 'City of God', chanting the Lord's praises constantly in his churches and with mankind living in virtue.

To that end, the Canons – who were subject to the onset of indolence like other men – had to be reformed from time to time, as with the monks. One such reform spread from Lorraine to Holland and thence to the abbey that Harold, later

The North Hall and its stately stairway porch, built in c. 1160–70 for pilgrims, Canterbury cathedral monastery. The hall, as usual with Norman domestic architecture, is on the upper floor (interior rebuilt in neo-Norman style), with an undercroft beneath

king, founded at Waltham Holy Cross, Essex, in 1061 (it was refounded as an establishment for Augustinian Canons by the Normans and its great Norman nave survives).

The other reform movement among the Canons was started in 1120 at Prémontré, near Lâon in France, by a group led by Norbert of Cologne who wanted to keep Augustine of Hippo's rule much more strictly. These Premonstratensian Canons in their turn started settlements elsewhere, including numerous new houses in England. Many existing Austin Canon establishments took up their severe rule too, including the priestly staff of Exeter cathedral.

The Norman gatehouse (completed in 1148) of the largely vanished Benedictine monastery of Bury St Edmunds, Suffolk. The finely executed late Norman motifs include two rows of billet-pattern around the entrance arch, fish-scale in the gable above, intersecting arcades and inventive motifs around the upper openings – all framed by strong plain buttresses

Like the monks' abbeys, the Austin Canons had their own chapter to govern each institution, so their buildings take a similar form to the Benedictine and other monasteries. Their houses were headed by a dean (whom they elected) or provost. If attached to an episcopal cathedral, they would leave the pastoral duties of the see to the bishop, his archdeacon and, later, the rural deans. They themselves were responsible for the cathedral services and they were financed by a system of 'prebends', each priest being supported by a particular estate or estates donated to the Church. Many of the great Norman cathedrals were run from the beginning on this system, notably St Paul's in London, and those at Exeter, Chichester, Lincoln, Hereford and York.

The finest remaining example of the Augustinian Canons' secular buildings at a cathedral are those at Bristol. The great cathedral church itself is all post-Norman now, and the remains of the Canons' day-to-day buildings are largely submerged in later additions. But they are exceptional in quality for their exuberant late Norman carved decoration.

Bristol cathedral was founded as an abbey of Reformed Augustinian Canons in 1142 by the Norman Robert fitz

Architecture of the Augustinian (Austin) Canons: the simple early Norman doorways and, beyond, more ornate entrance arches to the late Norman chapter house in the east range of the cloister, Bristol cathedral

Harding, later Lord Berkeley (who joined the house himself). The earliest remains form part of the completely Norman east range of the largely destroyed cloister. There is a series of simple doorways, of c. 1145, one of them opening on to the stairs up to the altered dormitory above. Beyond these doors, in the centre of the east range, is the entrance vestibule to the chapter house. This and all the other sumptuous Norman work at Bristol is of 1160–70.

To approach the late Norman parts around Bristol cathedral, it is best to start outside the precinct, at the main gatehouse. The upper part was rebuilt later, but the main and subsidiary arches are of c. 1170, with rib-vaulting inside, their ornament formed from spiral shafts with bands of intersected zigzag, arcading and lacing – some bands running continuously around each upright and arch in a way later typical of West Country Gothic. Beyond the gatehouse and a little down the hill, the doorway to the Dean's Lodging lies on the left, with similar rich motifs above simple shafts and a matching arch in the courtyard within (the upper part of the house has been altered). But it is the chapter house that is the extreme experience here; returning to the east range of the cloister, the arcaded vestibule penetrates into this extraordinarily decorated

A *chef d'oeuvre* of late Norman abstract architectural sculpture: the chapter house (c. 1160–70) of the Augustinian Canons at Bristol cathedral. One lunette panel has cable-patterned intersecting blank arcades, another multiple zigzag, and the vaulted ceiling has zigzagged ribs

space. Oblong in plan, its roof is vaulted with zigzagged and rosetted ribs, the walls rising over blank arcade chapter-seats to enriched intersecting arcades above and then lunette panels of multiple zigzag or blank arcading up into the vaults.

After this almost frenzied excitement of abstract ornament – of which glimpses can be seen at other Augustinian abbeys and priories such as Kirkham in North Yorkshire – the buildings of the reformed Premonstratensian Canons come as a calming sedative. A good late Norman example of this austere order of Canons can be seen at Dryburgh Abbey near St Boswell's in Borders Region, founded by King David I or his constable in 1150. The big round arches of the buildings in the cloister are certainly Romanesque, though Transitional motifs such as dog-tooth indicate that they are probably of a date nearer to 1190 than to the foundation date. Their restraint provides a good preface to the simplifying influence of the Cistercian order.

The Cistercians (called the White Monks, from their clothes) originated in 1098 when some French monks left a degenerate monastery in France and started yet another reformed order at Cîteaux (Cistercium in Latin). Their rule was drawn up by the Englishman Stephen Harding, but their

Detail of abstract wall-carving, of c. 1160–70, in the chapter house of Bristol cathedral. The tops of blank arcade seating can be seen below. Note the string-course and columns of cable-pattern with pellet motif between the strands, intersecting arcades, straight interlace and zigzagged panels above, the rib-vault springing from the corbel and the short half-pier

growth started with a great leader called St Bernard, who joined them in 1113. Bernard taught that they must settle in remote places, make their own clothes and grow their food by constant manual labour, maintain the *Opus Dei* with plain chant, have no ornament of clothing or building, eat only one meal a day (without meat or fish) and spend no time on scholarship. It was the hardest rule yet, but it fitted the pious revival then starting.

The first Cistercian settlement in Britain was in Dyfed, Wales, in about 1115. Then followed (in England) Waverley in Surrey, 1128, Tintern in Gwent, 1131, and (in Scotland) Melrose in the Borders, 1136; no Norman buildings remain at these sites now. But the Cistercians also began a long campaign of reinhabiting the north of England, still left barren from the Conqueror's slaughter of 1170. These Yorkshire monastery ruins are the finest of all in England: Rievaulx, founded in 1132, Fountains in 1133, Kirkstall outside Leeds in 1152, Jervaulx in 1156 and Byland in 1177. The pattern of each is similar, so the best-preserved, Fountains `Abbey, will be described here – though the others are just as rewarding to visit.

In 1132 the prior and sacrist of a worldly Benedictine

Architecture of the Premonstratensian Canons: simplified forms with round arches, thin roll-mouldings and a little dog-tooth ornament of c. 1190 in the cloister at Dryburgh Abbey, in the Borders of Scotland. The chapter house is on the right, with the entrance to the ruined abbey church on the left

A typical Cistercian
monastery plan

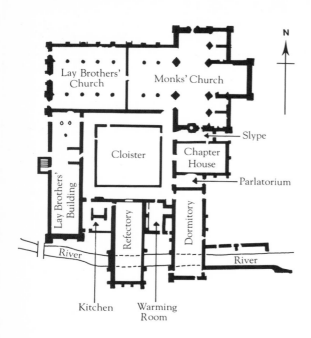

N

Lay Brothers'
Church

Monks' Church

Slype

Cloister

Chapter
House

Parlatorium

Lay Brothers'
Building

Refectory

Dormitory

River

River

Kitchen

Warming
Room

monastery in York led a group of dissatisfied monks on a
wandering route via Ripon to settle on land in Skelldale
provided by the archbishop. St Bernard sent them a Cistercian
monk from France to teach them the rule and in 1135 a
wealthy man joined the community. So the famous buildings
were started, the Norman and Transitional work continuing
until 1179. St Bernard's ban on the Cluniac type of
architectural enrichment was observed, but the Cistercian
masons' sheer grandeur of handling spaces and big architectural forms actually gains from that. The order introduced to
England the corbel (projecting from a wall to support
vaulting), the pointed arch (though still in walls of
Romanesque solidity, rather than Gothic lightness), the bell
capital (rather than the earlier Norman cuboid cushion form),
the rounded abacus above the capital and waterleaf decoration
on the capitals as the only sculpted ornament.

From the best approach to Fountains – the western
gatehouse (of indeterminate date) – a great open court reveals
the ruined abbey church on the left, with the roofless monastic
buildings ahead and on the right. Approaching these, their
monumental scale is awe-inspiring. On the right are two guest-
houses of c. 1170–1210, open to the sky now, like all except

the undercrofts. Ahead is the long rhythmic range of the lay-brothers' building of the 1170s, its south (right-hand) end their infirmary of c. 1205. (Lay-brothers were a Cistercian invention to gain extra help in running their farming without contravening Bernard's veto on involving outside servants as the Benedictines did.) There is a pretty bridge of the 1170s over the river on the right here.

The entrance to the monastery is by the archways through the lay-brothers' building – the famous vaulted undercroft was partly a cellar and partly their refectory, while the external stairway led up to their long dormitory above. The archways lead through the undercroft into the main cloister, whose four arcaded walks were probably of timber and so have disappeared.

Emerging into the cloister, one is in the monks' own quarters. The south side is on the right, with arches and blank arcades of the 1170s; in the middle of that side is the roofless monks' refectory of 1170–1205, the remains of their kitchen on its right, the well-preserved washroom or lavatorium on its left, with their warming room and the stairs to their vanished dormitory beyond (the monks' reredorter, stone water-closets, are built above the river to the south of this).

Returning to the cloister, the east side is opposite the entrance archway. In its centre is the entrance to the chapter house (of the 1160s, with shafts with waterleaf capitals, but its upper levels destroyed), to its left the slype or church-passage of the same date (later made into a library!), and to its right the parlatorium (where the monks could converse – vaulted, with pretty waterleaf corbels, again probably of the 1160s) leading to the undercroft of the monks' dormitory and the later, more ruinous, buildings beyond.

On the other, northern, side of the cloister lies the roofless abbey church itself. In terms of architectural history its nave is particularly significant, for it is probably the earliest part of the monastery and its Anglo-Norman piers are topped by typically Cistercian pointed arches built as early as c. 1135–47 (the east part of the church and its tower are much later, of the early 1200s and 1520s).

In all, the Cistercians had founded sixty-three monasteries in England by the year 1200 and had much influence on the country's architectural development and monastic life. They did not remain the most austere order for long, for in 1180 King Henry II founded a house at Witham in Somerset (a chapel and a dovecot remain) of the solitary Carthusian monks

Fountains Abbey, N. Yorkshire. *Left:* Cistercian monastery architecture, monumental but undecorated: the entrance to the lay-brothers' building (1170s), with the stairway up to their dormitory

Below left: The long rib-vaulted undercroft of the lay-brothers' building, with some of the pointed arches introduced to England by this reformed order of monks

Right: Two further architectural innovations of the Cistercian monks, in the parlatorium of c. 1150–60: the corbel to support roof vaulting ribs; the waterleaf capital

Above: The east side of the cloister (its presumably wooden arcaded walks now destroyed). On the left is the entrance to the slype; the central three doorways lead to the chapter house; on the right is the parlatorium.

(an order founded at St Bruno's Grande Chartreuse near Grenoble in 1084, though its communities, with separate dwellings and gardens for each brother, spread slowly). The Charterhouses' influence in England – apart from the Carthusian St Hugh, Bishop of Lincoln – lies beyond the twelfth century, as does that of the Franciscan and Dominican Friars, established after 1210. One final order of English monks and nuns should be mentioned, however – that of St Gilbert of Sempringham. At Old Malton in North Yorkshire there are the best ruins of one of the fourteen Gilbertian houses, which contained some 1,000 nuns and 500 monks between them (together but segregated), that Gilbert founded before his death in 1199.

Suggestions for Travellers

As will be seen from the maps with this guide, there are interesting traces of one or two monasteries of the Norman period in many counties. But only in Kent, Shropshire, northern Norfolk, the Borders of Scotland and – most of all – Yorkshire are there several sites with enough remains to evoke the vanished grandeur of the monks, nuns and Canons.

6

NORMAN CATHEDRALS AND ABBEY CHURCHES

Whatever the splendours and fascination of buildings put up before and since the twelfth century, it seems inescapable that the greatest architectural works in Britain are the thirty or so cathedrals and major abbey churches started by the Anglo-Normans. Some of them were wholly or in part rebuilt in Gothic styles within three centuries, but many remain substantially intact or the Norman work forms a major part of a blend of the periods. In all these great churches the level of architectural achievement varies, yet the overall handling of great spaces within massive stone forms is on an extraordinarily high level. The development of this feeling for enclosed space will be traced here, as well as the growth of carved ornament – abstract and figure sculpture.

As observed in the chapter on small churches, the Normans had already formed their own disciplined brand of Romanesque architecture and were building half a dozen big abbey churches in Normandy at the time of the Conquest. William I had a good relationship with the Papacy, without the frictions between Church and State that brought the Holy Roman Emperor to kneel in the snow before the Pope at Canossa in 1076. In the dispute over the political supremacy of pope or king, the Norman ruler accepted a general duty of obedience, but Rome was forced to accept that he continued to appoint his own archbishops and bishops. William, growing fat and bald as he aged, never lost his foresight and stony will in building the Crown's lasting control of England.

The appointment of these bishops was important to William in two ways. In all feudal countries the bishops owed service of knights and taxes to their king, just as the barons did, for the Church controlled around a quarter of all land and on it had wide powers. In newly conquered England, they were especially important to the king – Edward the Confessor had already appointed some able Normans to vacant sees, but within a few years, William had his own countrymen in every English bishopric except Worcester.

In this change of church control, William had the resolute help of the formidable Lanfranc, Papal Legate and from 1070 to 1089 Archbishop of Canterbury. In 1075 Lanfranc called the first of a series of councils in London, instructed the bishops to move their seats from the isolated Anglo-Saxon locations to their biggest towns, and started the campaign of new cathedral building. Among others, the East Anglian seat was moved from Anglo-Saxon North Elmham to Thetford and then to Norwich, the Wessex seat from Sherborne to Old Sarum (later Salisbury), and the seat of the huge see stretching from Oxfordshire to the Humber was moved from Dorchester to Lincoln. Some of the new cathedrals were to be staffed by Benedictine monks, while others – including those at Lincoln, London, Chichester and Sarum – were run by Canons (see Chapter 5). Work on the new cathedrals soon started and even at Worcester the sole Anglo-Saxon bishop, Wulfstan, co-

Early Norman cathedral architecture: the crossing of St Albans Abbey (later cathedral), Hertfordshire, of 1077–88. The central tower and its daylit inner lantern is supported on lofty and massive double-stepped arches, decorated only by simple red and white patterns painted on to the whitewashed stone

operated, recording sadly that he set about pulling down the cathedral of his ancestors.

Many of these early cathedrals, and the other monastic abbey churches started at the same time, were rebuilt even before the end of the Norman Romanesque period in about 1200. At some, such as Canterbury and Rochester, little but the early crypts remain. St Albans, shrine of the first British martyr, is the only one of the great churches started in the 1070s and 80s where the almost military early Norman tower and much of the outer walls of chancel, transepts and nave can still be seen. The interior of these is preserved at St Albans too, all dating from 1077 to 1088. The lofty spaces of the crossing,

One of the early Norman transepts (1079–c. 1100) of Winchester cathedral, Hampshire. It is decoratively simple in the extreme, but of masterly spatial complexity

and the four areas opening off it, are held in primitively strong architectural masses – there is no sculptural ornament beyond the double stepping of the arches and a few re-used Saxon baluster-shafts. The walls were whitewashed from the start, but perhaps around 1110 the arches were relieved of some severity by painted checkering and other patterns.

Great architecture, of course, is primarily a matter of spaces, solid forms and proportions, with detail and decoration the secondary constituents. One gets some glimpse of the possibilities of unornamented early Norman stone design in the movingly noble spaces of the transepts which are all that remain of the cathedral of 1079–c. 1100 at Winchester, the ancient Anglo-Saxon capital. These are the finest achievement of Lanfranc's building campaign and one regrets the loss of the rest of the building, despite the Gothic beauty that replaced it. Yet a very similar style, in the hands of some lesser designer, produced the surviving nave of Blyth Priory (Nottinghamshire) in 1088–c. 1100, speaking of a grim disciplined Norman God without the grace expressed at Winchester. And on the voluted capitals of the Blyth arcade there are examples of early Norman figure sculpture, its crudity typical of the conquerors until well into the 1100s.

Below: The largely Norman exterior of Norwich cathedral, the south transept on the right (c. 1105–20), central tower (lower part c. 1120, higher levels c. 1140), and nave on the left (c. 1118–45, a few windows since altered)

Right: The chancel and apsed east end (1096–c. 1110), with composite piers, billet carving on the lower arches and roll-moulding on those above

Below right: Plan of Norwich cathedral, largely as it is still with its eastern apse (some apsed chapels rebuilt)

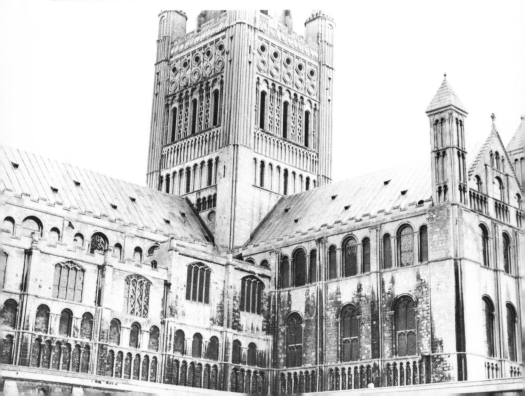

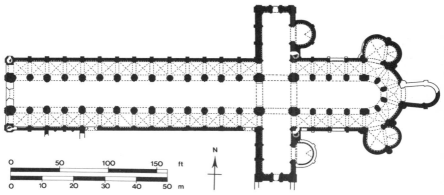

At the end of the 1000s Anglo-Norman mastery of Romanesque design took a major step forward. Several more cathedrals were started during the 1090s, though survivors of that decade are still rare – churches were almost always started at the chancel (then invariably apsed) for the altar and the priests, and it is these east ends that were most frequently rebuilt with changing fashions. But one example remains almost intact, and that is one of the two most beautiful of Norman cathedrals, at Norwich.

Norwich cathedral was started in 1096 and most of its exterior, including the tower below the famous spire, is obviously of between that date and 1150. The earliest part of the interior is the gracefully apsed chancel, completed in c. 1110, providing an intensely satisfying climax to the visitor's lengthy progress along the nave (c. 1118–45, with serene arcades with zigzag ornament, unlike the apse) and under the soaring lantern of the crossing (built c. 1105–20, with the transepts). There is a new enlightenment of spirit in the feelings aroused by these spaces, which have a particularly Romanesque eloquence, with a changed and more open relationship of voids to the solid masses typical of the style in its earlier Norman phases.

Just beside the crossing at Norwich, two great drum-piers, carved with incised spirals, face each other across the nave. These date fairly precisely the start of building the nave, for they must represent a plan (afterwards abandoned) to erect a nave in the new, very English, Norman style of Durham. Durham cathedral, the thunderous masterpiece of Romanesque architecture in western Europe, was a new building started in 1093 to provide a major religious centre for the north beyond York, and a shrine for the miracle-working relics of St Cuthbert of Lindisfarne (see Chapter 1).

The distant impact of the cathedral, on its peninsula rock in a meander of the river, is matched by the majesty of its interior – not military as is St Albans, but seeming to express a deity of limitless mystery and power. The chancel was completed with its rib-vault by about 1104 (the east end was rebuilt, but beautifully, in the Gothic style of c. 1250), the crossing and north transept by 1110, and the south transept and then the celebrated nave were started in c. 1110 and ready by 1133. Later in the Norman period, the west towers were built by c. 1140 and the Galilee Chapel (with the bones of the Jarrow historian Bede) in the lighter and ornate manner of c. 1170. Apart from the west window and the extreme east end of the church, the fifteenth-century central tower is the only major post-Norman work.

Large-scale rib-vaulting in England starts with the Durham chancel. The incised drum-piers of the nave and its zigzag carved ornament were also new features seized on by masons from all parts of England. The zigzag or chevron motif, with many later-developed forms, became the typical Anglo-Norman decoration. The incised piers are a more ambitious and rarer feature; their brief appearance at Norwich in c. 1118 has been mentioned, as have the few cases in parish churches (see Chapter 3). But some other major abbey churches have arcades with such carved drums, always with an effect of splendour that seems to enrich the space around them as well as their own surfaces. Such arcades can be seen at Selby Abbey in North Yorkshire, Waltham Cross just outside London in Essex, and most impressively of all at Scotland's greatest abbey, Dunfermline in Fife. Finally, there is a ruined arcade with incised drum-piers at Lindisfarne Abbey on Holy Island, Northumberland. All these date from c. 1120, with Dunfermline perhaps the latest at 1128–c. 50.

Drum-piers themselves, however, without the incised patterns and in continuous rows (rather than alternating with composite shafted piers, in the Durham style) appear in a larger group of big Norman churches. They seem to originate in the West Country, in an extraordinarily tall form, along the naves built in c. 1100–20 at Gloucester cathedral and Tewkesbury Abbey. Such very high piers open up the

Plan of Durham cathedral, showing the original apsed east end (now rebuilt differently)

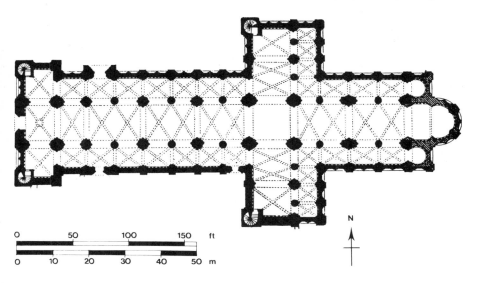

0   50   100   150   ft

0 10 20 30 40 50 m

N

Durham cathedral, built in 1093–c. 1140, including the west towers (the low west Galilee Chapel seen here was added in c. 1170, and the large west window and tall central tower was rebuilt later)

Below: The nave roof of Durham cathedral, with zigzag ornamented rib-vaulting of c. 1125–33. The diagonal ribs spring from corbels

apparent breadth and flow of space sideways into the aisles,
though leaving room for only a rather pinched gallery between
the main arcade and the clerestory above.

After Gloucester and Tewkesbury, masons elsewhere in the
country used the round-pier motif in some of the finest of the
great abbeys – the naves at Southwell in Nottinghamshire
(c. 1120–40, in a mighty and almost intact Norman church) and
Leominster in Hereford and Worcester (1121–c. 50), and the
surviving apsed chancel at St Bartholomew-the-Great in
London (1123–c. 40) all have this feature, experimenting
with various pier and gallery height ratios. The series comes to
its peak achievement with Romsey Abbey in Hampshire,
where the Benedictine nuns built a serenely soaring church,
delectably detailed, in c. 1130–60.

Most of these round-piered churches were started within
the prosperous and civilising order of Henry I's reign. That
king – so different from his father William I, except in his squat

figure and his talent for organising and administering the
kingdom – was an urbane, stingy and sensuous man who
preferred law-making and mistresses to the battle-field.
Merchants and farmers prospered in his long reign from 1100
to 1135, and so did the Church after his early confrontations
with Archbishop Anselm were resolved in 1107.

It was Henry I who built the big Norman keep in one corner
of the ruined Roman fortress at Portchester, Hampshire, and
he went on to establish in 1133 an Augustinian priory in
another angle of the huge Roman enclosure. This cruciform
priory church is still almost intact, composed of fine simple
forms, and is untouched by the new fashion for rich sculpture
starting then. But that was fairly typical of priory churches of
that time. The two loveliest Norman churches in Wales make
the point well: the chancel of Ewenny Priory in Mid
Glamorgan (nave built in c. 1120, chancel in c. 1140), with its

The tall plain drum-
piers of Gloucester
cathedral nave,
c. 1105–20. The
soffits of the arches
have two roll-
mouldings, and the
extrados are stepped
and then zigzagged (as
are the diminutive
gallery arches above).
The rib-vaulted roof
is post-Norman

Left: The nave of Romsey Abbey, Hampshire (c. 1130–60). This lofty interior combines strong forms with unusual and delicate detail

Right: One of the two Norman west towers, the nave, transepts and central crossing tower of Southwell Minster, Nottinghamshire (c. 1120–40). This is a rare example of a largely intact Norman exterior on a major scale, its impact derived from majestic proportions rather than from the sparse carved ornament

Below: The ribbed barrel-vaulted chancel of Ewenny Priory church, Mid Glamorgan (c. 1120–40). It is spatially outstanding, with minimum roll-moulding and zigzag ornament for its date

simple beauty of form and space, and all but the north transept of Penmon Priory in Anglesey (c. 1120–50) have but the slightest ornament. Only in the Penmon transept of c. 1150–70 does the ornate multiple zigzag and other decoration burst out.

The new cathedral started during Henry I's peaceful reign was Peterborough in 1118–43, its nave done by 1190. Like Norwich, the apsed chancel, crossing, transepts and nave form an impressively complete Norman interior, though the level of spatial inspiration is not so intense in this design. Like some rows of late Georgian houses, one feels that an approved pattern has set in. Any danger of that happening at Ely, where the nave and transepts are of c. 1100–40 (the earlier chancel has gone), is countered by the brilliant west tower of c. 1140–50 (as well as by the famous octagon of 1320 that replaced the fallen Norman crossing tower).

A later Norman cathedral: the chancel and apse, Peterborough cathedral, Cambridgeshire (c. 1118–90)

The revival of figure sculpture in the 1140s: a relief-sculpted panel on the Norman west front of Lincoln cathedral, recounting the stories of Noah and of Daniel with the lions

The tower at Ely is outstanding among Norman decorative dramatisations of wide stone surfaces though there are other impressive examples of this talent on the cathedrals of Rochester (the west front, 1140–50), Lincoln (the lower part of the west towers, 1140–50) and Exeter (the towers, uniquely over the transepts, c. 1170s). Lincoln west front is a mêlée of early Norman (the four tall arches are of c. 1090), later Norman (the three enriched porticos and sculpted bands are of c. 1140) and Gothic traceried windows inserted later. But the appearance of expressive if naïve figure sculpture here is probably among the earliest in Anglo-Norman architecture.

The bands of panels at Lincoln tell biblical stories with much impact – Daniel in the lions' den, Noah's ark and others. The detailed carving is fine. It may be that the sculpted capitals removed from William II's Westminster Hall, when it was rebuilt, were of the 1090s, but it is more likely they were added later. The same applies to the famous capitals still in the crypt at Canterbury, for they too seem likely to have been carved in c. 1140 when the French revival in sculpture is known to have reached England. Certainly, the brilliant Herefordshire school of architectural sculpture arose shortly after that, perhaps spurred by the arrival of a mason taught at Canterbury or elsewhere, and the west portal of Leominster Abbey may date from about this time (see Chapter 3 for an account of ornamental development).

Hereford cathedral (started with its chancel of c. 1115–30,

followed by its crossing nave of c. 1130–45) is a notable building for tracing the development of late Norman sculptural ornament of that county's typical almost Celtic character (though it was abstract, unlike the beakhead and figure sculpture of parish churches such as nearby Kilpeck). The chancel (its apse, beyond the big eastern arch, has gone now) has zigzag in all sorts of varieties, while the nave takes zigzag even further and adds transverse mouldings and interlace capitals (but one should be rather wary of the restoration of 1843 here).

Moving into Scotland, where the Normalised King David I brought in feudalism and Romanesque architecture during his reign of 1124–53, Durham-type zigzag appears in the ruined chancel and crossing of Jedburgh Abbey (Augustinian) in the Borders. But the museum in the abbey's grounds reveals nothing Norman that is as finely carved as one pre-Conquest Northumbrian fragment there. The large-scale early Scottish churches are scattered in time across the Norman period, though all bar those at Dunfermline and Kirkwall are in ruins. The vast St Andrews cathedral in Fife was built from 1160 onwards and there are quite sophisticated Norman Romanesque features among its spectacular remains. Kelso, in the Borders, is the astonishing shadow of an abbey church of yet another reformed order of the Benedictines, the Tironensians, brought here from France – perhaps to initiate the Auld Alliance – by David I in 1126. A plan discovered in the Vatican has revealed that this ruin is the west end of a long double-cruciform church. The style is curious, for there are eroded traces of ornate portals, enriched intersected arcading, pointed arches and (in one transept) waterleaf capitals – all adding up to a probable date in Scotland of c. 1180–1200.

Two major Scottish cathedrals to note are in Orkney, off the mainstream course of British history. Birsay cathedral is a scant fragment of Earl Thorfinn's church of c. 1050–90. The other is Kirkwall cathedral, started by the Norse Earl Rognvald, ruler of these northern islands in 1137, in memory of his martyred uncle, Magnus. The cathedral is small, built of local red sandstone, and despite its 300 years of building, the interior is entirely in a simplified and endearing Norman Romanesque style and still well worth a pilgrimage.

In England there are two Norman cathedrals showing very different aspects of late Romanesque. Oxford cathedral, built as an abbey church, was apparently completed from chancel to west end in c. 1180–1210: it is quite small and very cool in the spatial expression of its round-piered arcades and squared-off east end (though given warmth by the late Gothic vaulting added above). The other late work, at Canterbury, will be described last of all.

In Wales, although there are some Norman traces at Llandaff cathedral, Cardiff, the great work is the nave of St David's. Here the cathedral's chancel and crossing, started in 1176, were destroyed, but the nave (probably of c. 1190–8) survives – very broad for its height and with the conventional zigzag decoration transformed into almost detached tendrilly tubes, with lozenges and key-pattern.

Does one detect a slackening of inspiration in these late Norman spaces? Compared with the cathedrals at Norwich and Durham, certainly. But then they were being built at a time when not just the pointed Gothic arch, but the Gothic feeling for space and wall was already present in England. This Transitional architecture can be traced in many churches. Among them, the abbey churches at Fountains (probably of 1135–47) and Rievaulx brought the pointed arcade arch, though with Romanesque piers and walls. At Wimborne Minster in Dorset, the nave arcades of c. 1170–80 have zigzagged pointed arches below and a round-topped gallery

Late Norman Romanesque: the chancel of Oxford cathedral (c. 1180–1210), with formalised but accomplished design and carved ornament. The roof vaulting and the tracery of the rose window were added later

above. By c. 1190–1210 the stupendous church of St Cross, in the southern outskirts of Winchester, was made electric by the combination of extreme zigzag and enriched intersected arcading with pointed arches in the (presumably) earlier lower arcades and rounded arches above – there are even windows that have both round and pointed arches over the same opening.

At St Cross one might want to rest this account, for the Transitional has nothing finer to offer. But the great church remains at heart Romanesque and the last word must be with Canterbury cathedral. It is here that one sees the early invasion of real Gothic feeling. The choir that Archbishop Anselm started in 1096 was completed in 1130, and in it the knights of the second great order-bringing King Henry murdered Archbishop Thomas à Becket in 1170. But four years later the whole main inner part of that choir was gutted by fire. In 1175 the French master-mason William de Sens started to reconstruct its roof and east end in the earliest truly Gothic style – with visually-light walls, piers and vaulting as well as pointed arches. The difference can be seen today by comparing the choir aisle (c. 1100–30) with the upper parts and east end

The last masterpiece of Romanesque architecture on a grand scale in England: St Cross Hospital church of c. 1190–1210, on the outskirts of Winchester. Spatially intense, it is made more intense by complex carved decoration and the unexpected combinations of pointed with rounded arches of the choir itself (1175 onwards).

The French mason's work was taken over by another, called William the Englishman. By 1184 this designer had extended the chancel eastwards into its present striking bell-like plan, added a new easterly crypt beneath and constructed an eastmost Lady Chapel, the tall round 'Corona' Chapel. Comparing this with St Cross the real transition is apparent: while St Cross has apparently Gothic features in forceful Romanesque forms, the Canterbury Corona Chapel has a little Anglo-Norman zigzag and some round arches on light shafts and soaring forms that foretell the Early English Gothic of Wells and Salisbury cathedrals.

This foretaste of the end of Anglo-Norman Romanesque in the 1180s went with wider changes. After more than a century, Anglo-Saxons and Normans were coming together – even their names and their languages were starting the merging that would be consummated in Chaucer's time. And an Englishman of Norman descent, Richard fitz Nigel, could write in the late 1100s, 'Now that English and Normans live close to each other, and marry each other, the nationalities are so merged that it is difficult to say, among free people, who is born English and who Norman.'

The transition from Anglo-Norman Romanesque to Gothic at Canterbury cathedral: on the right, the zigzagged rounded arches over the aisle around St Anselm's choir (1096–1130, largely destroyed by fire 1174); on the left, the early Gothic vaulted choir itself, as rebuilt by the French mason William de Sens in 1175 onwards

Suggestions for Travellers

The great Norman cathedrals and abbey churches were distributed all over southern England and more thinly in the north, in Scotland and in southern Wales. South of the Thames, Canterbury and Winchester cathedrals have important eleventh-century architecture remaining among the Gothic, while those at Chichester, Rochester, Romsey and St Cross are substantially and gloriously Norman. On the northern side of the Thames valley, St Albans is mostly early Norman and Oxford late Norman, while the nave of Waltham Abbey and the chancel of St Bartholomew's in London are eloquent examples of the 1120s. The fen country and East Anglia have three great cathedrals: Ely is Norman from the crossing westwards; Norwich is entirely a masterpiece of the early 1100s; and Peterborough has a complete interior only a little later. The south-west has only the twin towers of Exeter cathedral dating from this period, but further north in the West Country are the vast Norman splendours of Gloucester, Tewkesbury and Hereford, plus parts of Worcester. In southern Wales scant traces survive of Norman work at Llandaff, but far in the west is the extraordinary late Norman St David's. In northern England on the west there are only the Norman crossing and transepts of Carlisle and minor parts of Chester among later Gothic rebuilding of the cathedrals. But on the eastern side, fragments of Lincoln and most of Southwell, Blyth, Selby and Ripon are Norman, early or late. Best of all, further north still, there is the superb cathedral of Durham. Beyond that lie the ruined Norman abbeys of the Borders, the splendours of Dunfermline, the ruins of St Andrews, the towers of Dunblane and Restenneth and the complete Romanesque cathedral of Kirkwall in distant Orkney.

GAZETTEER

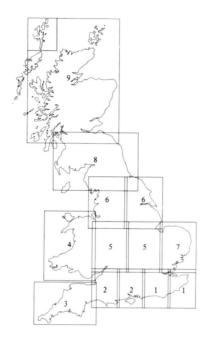

Key to symbols

✠ cathedral or major abbey church

⛊ castle or fort

⛌ Anglo-Saxon church (or substantial parts)

⌂ house (or substantial parts), Norman or earlier

✚ Norman or largely Norman church

■ other Anglo-Saxon, Celtic, etc. monument

⊕ Anglo-Saxon or Celtic monastery remains

⊙ town with several Anglo-Saxon or Norman buildings

⊕ Norman monastery ruins

○ modern town

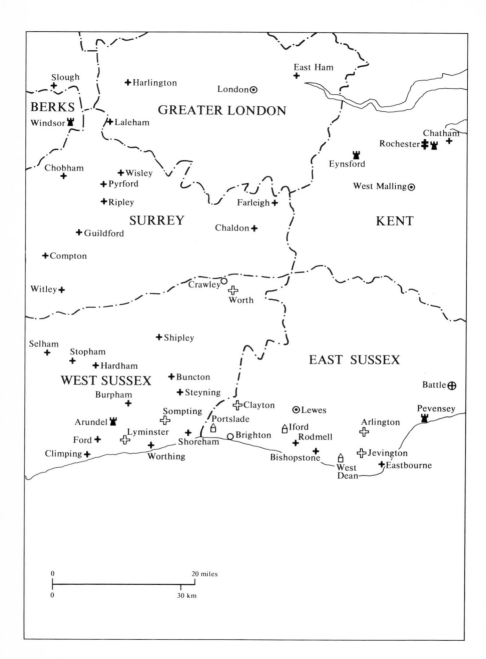

1 South-East England

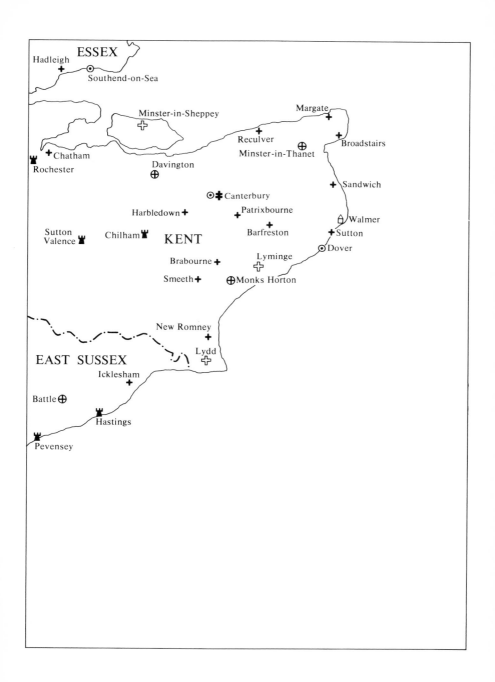

ESSEX

Hadleigh

Southend-on-Sea

Minster-in-Sheppey

Margate

Reculver

Broadstairs

Minster-in-Thanet

Chatham

Davington

Rochester

Sandwich

Canterbury

Harbledown

Patrixbourne

Walmer

Barfreston

Sutton

Sutton
Valence

Chilham

KENT

Dover

Brabourne

Lyminge

Smeeth

Monks Horton

New Romney

EAST SUSSEX

Lydd

Icklesham

Battle

Hastings

Pevensey

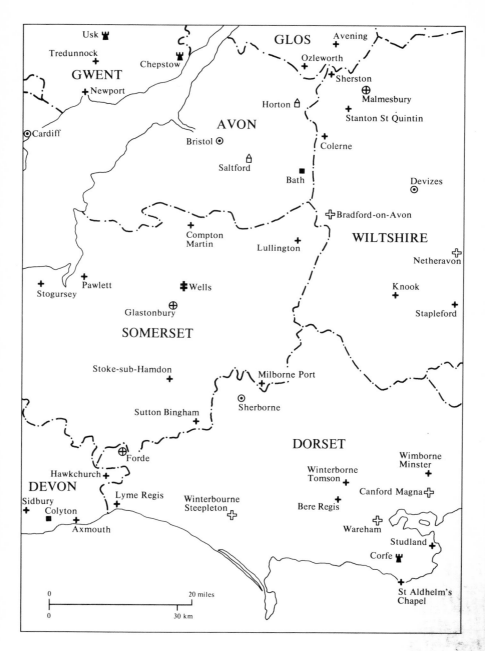

2 Southern England

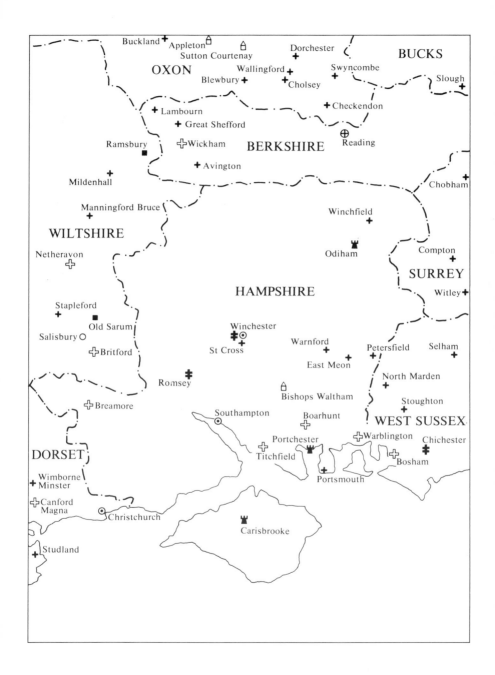

3 South-West England

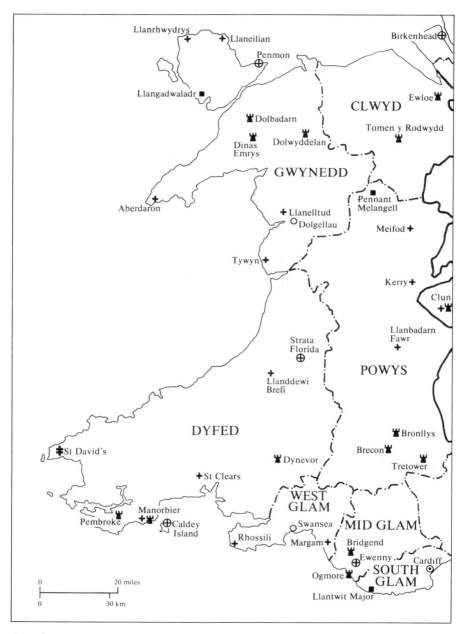

4 Wales

5 Midlands

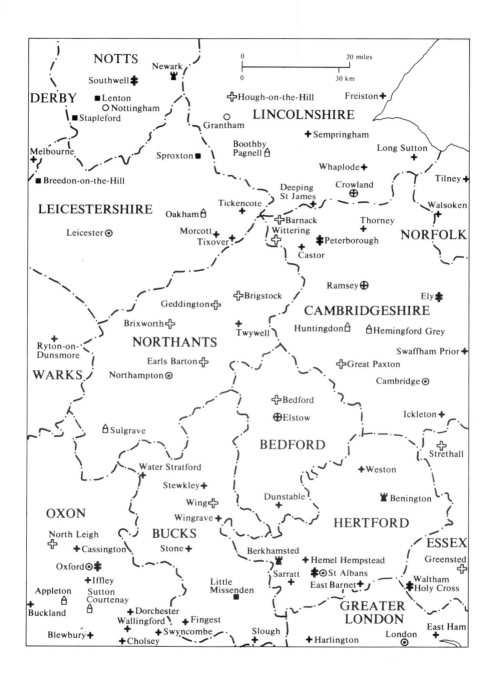

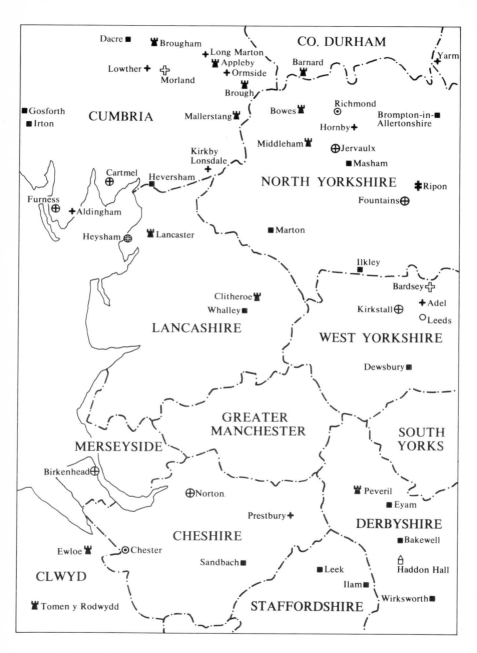

6 Northern England

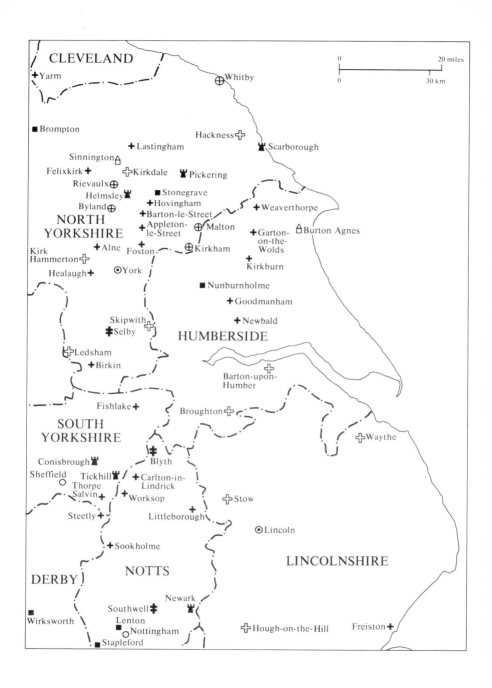

CLEVELAND

+Yarm

0 _____ 20 miles
0 _____ 30 km

⊕Whitby

■ Brompton

Hackness⊹
+Lastingham

Scarborough

Sinnington⌂
Felixkirk +
⊹Kirkdale

Rievaulx⊕
Helmsley✠
Byland⊕

NORTH
YORKSHIRE

Pickering

■Stonegrave
+Hovingham
+Barton-le-Street
Appleton-
le-Street

+Weaverthorpe

⊕Malton

⊟Burton Agnes
+Garton-
on-the-
Wolds

+Alne
Foston

⊕Kirkham

Kirk
Hammerton⊹

Healaugh +

⊙York

+Kirkburn

■ Nunburnholme

+Goodmanham

Skipwith
✠Selby

⊹

HUMBERSIDE

+Newbald

⊹Ledsham
+Birkin

⊹
Barton-upon-
Humber

Fishlake +

Broughton⊹

SOUTH
YORKSHIRE

⊹Waythe

Conisbrough✠
Sheffield ○
Tickhill✠
Thorpe
Salvin +
✠
Blyth
+Carlton-in-
Lindrick
+Worksop

⊹Stow

+
Steetly +
Littleborough

⊙Lincoln

+Sookholme

LINCOLNSHIRE

NOTTS

DERBY

Newark

Southwell✠
■
Wirksworth
Lenton
○Nottingham

■
Stapleford

✠
✠Hough-on-the-Hill

Freiston+

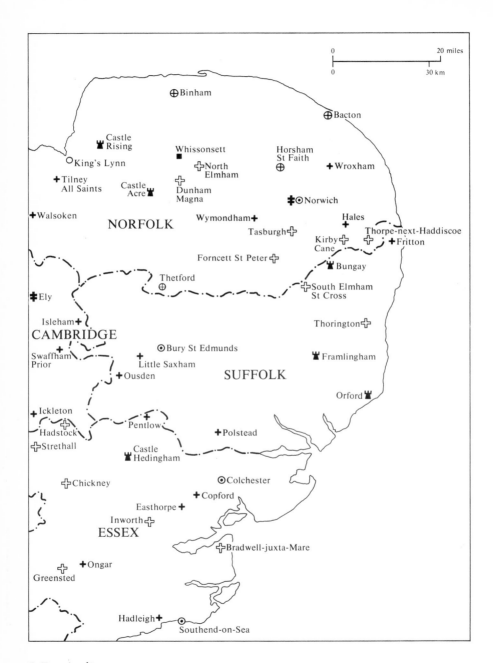

7 East Anglia

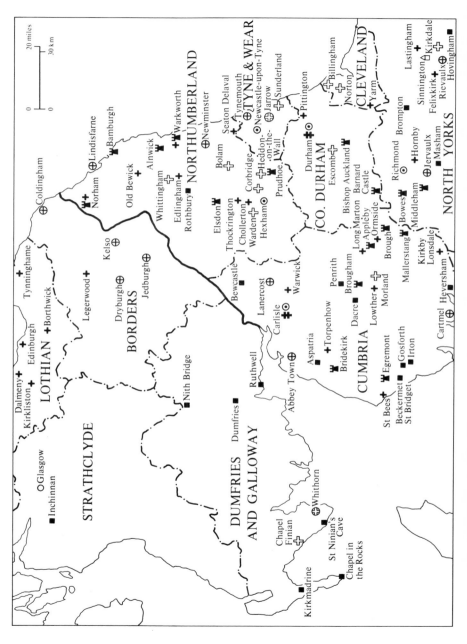

8 Border Country and Southern Scotland

9 Northern Scotland

GAZETTEER

The buildings included here have been selected as those of the period most rewarding to visit – many other buildings in Britain have some Anglo-Saxon or Norman features. Places (or, if remotely sited in the countryside, individual buildings) are listed in alphabetical order throughout Great Britain and its offshore islands. Listed entries are marked on the maps, with symbols for each type of building or for towns with more than one building of the period worth visiting. In the notes with each gazetteer entry, centuries are sometimes indicated as, for example, C12 for the twelfth century. Very few exact dates are known for Anglo-Saxon or Norman buildings, so most dates are given as, for example, c. 1160, based on stylistic or sometimes documentary evidence.

Pages of the main text bearing direct reference to the subject of each entry are indicated in brackets (italicised page numbers refer to illustrations).

Abbey Dore, Hereford and Worcester. Cistercian *abbey church* of which only chancel, crossing (tower much later) and transepts, c. 1180–1210, now exist as parish church. Transitional style, Cistercian-type rib-vaulting, pointed arches, waterleaf and then stiff-leaf capitals, etc. Scanty fragments of monastic buildings.
Abbey Town, Cumbria. *Holme Cultram*

Abbey church is the W front and nave, c. 1180, of Cistercian monastery founded from Melrose in Scotland. Pointed arches and waterleaf capitals, etc.
Aberdaron, Gwynedd. *Church* has Norman W front and N arcade in nave. Overlooks pilgrims' embarkation point for Bardsey Island – Ynys Enlli – the holy 'isle of 20,000 saints' (the monks buried there) where nothing remains but the atmosphere.
Aberdeen, Grampian Region. *St Nicholas,* with many features of ambitious cruciform Norman church, with aisled nave, though mostly rebuilt.
Aberdour, Fife Region. *Church* is basically Romanesque, C12, much altered.
Aberlemno, Tayside Region. Roadside *cross,* c. 900, and earlier Pictish symbol *stones.*
Abernethy, Tayside Region. On the border of Tayside and Fife. In churchyard, a high *round tower* (40, 67), like that at Brechin (q.v.), but rather later. Lower 12 courses of stone, c. 1050, the lofty higher parts perhaps some decades later.
Adel, West Yorkshire. In northern outer suburb of Leeds, a small, ornamented and largely complete Norman *church.* Nave and square-ended chancel only. Fine corbel-table and eroded gable sculpture outside. 4-order doorway with animals and zigzag. Enriched chancel arch with figure-sculpted capitals. All c. 1160.
Aldingham, Cumbria. *Church,* nave with arcade, c. 1190, with handsome later chancel, overlooking sea.
Alne, North Yorkshire. Tower, chancel and nave of *church,* c. 1100 (but many features altered). Some good carving, notably S door, c. 1180.
Alnwick, Northumberland. *Castle,* Norman shell-keep of c. 1150, with zigzagged entrance arch, still there among the extravaganzas of C14, C18 and C19 Percys, Dukes of Northumberland. *Abbey,* little remains of the Premonstratensians' great foundation of 1147, and less still is Norman.
Appleby, Cumbria. *Castle,* its attractive square keep (48), c. 1180, with restored and pretty turrets added C17 by that great preserver of Cumbrian castles, Lady Anne Clifford. *Church,* post-Norman, but has Anglo-Norse carved hogback tombstones preserved.
Appleton, Oxfordshire. *Appleton*

Manor, c. 1200, with splendid round-arched Transitional doorway. Inside this, hall partly survives (alterations include Tudor fireplace) with 2 internal Norman doorways. *Church* nearby has Transitional arcade, c. 1190.

Appleton-le-Street, North Yorkshire. *Church tower*, 900s, heightened in c. 1100. W door, c. 1180, with waterleaf; the rest C13.

Arlington, East Sussex. *Church* has Saxon nave, with long-and-short work quoins, and Norman chapel.

Arundel, West Sussex. *Castle*, with inner gatehouse and motte of c. 1080s. On motte, Henry II's shell-keep (45) of 1170s, with 1 richly zigzagged doorway, other Norman doors and features including well and tunnel-vaulted storeroom. Hidden away, vaulted undercroft of Henry II's Great Hall and apartments (rebuilt). All this among the Dukes of Norfolk's extravaganzas of 1791 and 1890.

Aspatria, Cumbria. *St Kentigern* (part Norman, part C19), some good Anglo-Danish hogback sculpted stones and other fragments.

Astley, Hereford and Worcester. *Church* has large Norman nave, c. 1160, with much later work.

Aston Eyre, Shropshire. Norman *church*, c. 1150–90, has glorious carved tympanum.

Avening, Gloucestershire. Cruciform *church*, c. 1100, nave with later Norman arcade, central tower, finely carved N doorway, c. 1160. Much work post-Norman and well restored from ruin by Micklethwaite, 1902.

Avington, Berkshire. Lovely and almost complete Norman *church*, though former chancel vaulting destroyed. Nave, chancel arch, chancel, with most of their original windows. All c. 1160 with much decorative carving.

Axmouth, Devon. *Church* has good S doorway, c. 1140, zigzagged and battlement-patterned orders of arch, plus Norman walls among later work inside.

Bacton, Norfolk. Ruins of *Broomholm Priory* (Cluniac branch of Benedictine) include remains of Norman church transept, chapel and dormitory among later work.

Bakewell, Derbyshire. In churchyard, the stump of a *cross* (23) with eroded sculpture and vine carving, c. 800. *Church* has fragments of Anglo-Saxon

and Norman sculpture. W front, c. 1150, much altered, beakhead and intersecting arcade, plus some features inside; the rest C13, etc.

Bamburgh, Northumberland. *Castle* (48), one of the most spectacular of England, on great shoreside rock. 3-storey hall-keep built c. 1130–50 (perhaps by King Stephen, no documents survive), its pitched roof replaced by 4th storey later. Chapel and part of entrance gateway of same date, outer walls and tower C13.

Bardsey, West Yorkshire. *Church*, tall tower Anglo-Saxon, nave now with Norman arcades of c. 1150 and 1190, enriched doorway, c. 1150, chancel C14. At Collingham, 1 mile NE of Bardsey, *church* (27), partly Norman, contains Anglian sculpture including Apostles' Cross, c. 800.

Barfreston, Kent. Tiny *church* (75), nave and chancel, zigzagged chancel arch, band on walls, etc. Dog-toothed nave window arches inside. Traces of original all-over wall-painting. Outside, main door, E end, etc., have magnificent sculptural decoration of c. 1190 (see waterleaf detail motif).

Barnack, Cambridgeshire. *Church*, tower of c. 1020, with typical late Anglo-Saxon long-and-short work quoins and lesene-strip decoration (spire C13). More Saxon traces in nave, but its arcades are Norman, c. 1180–1200, Transitional arches. Fine carving of seated Christ, c. 1020.

Barnard Castle, County Durham. Round keep (55), built by Baliol family (founders of Baliol College, Oxford, and one of them a King of Scotland), c. 1200 or after; the rest later.

Barrow, Shropshire. Fascinating *church*, chancel and chancel arch Anglo-Saxon, c. 1040–50; the rest austere early Norman, c. 1100.

Barton-le-Street, North Yorkshire. Little Norman *church* with superb carving (S door, corbel-table and inside) c. 1160, but much of it C19 restoration.

Barton-upon-Humber, Humberside. Major Anglo-Saxon church of *St Peter* (36,36) (a fine Gothic church stands on other side of the town pond). W forebuilding beside tower believed to be of c. 950, the famous tower itself (whose interior acted as the nave) c. 990, with elaborate lesenes or pilaster-strips up its flanks. Anglian chancel to E of tower replaced by present large church (nave and chancel), C13.

Bath, Avon. *Abbey church,* 1499 onwards, replacing Norman abbey, but some expressive figure-sculpted capitals, etc., of 1140s shown in choir vestry off S aisle.

Battle Abbey, East Sussex. Of the Benedictine abbey (94) founded by William I on site of Battle of Hastings, only an early Norman arch, many foundations, etc., and a notable C13 dormitory survived the destruction of 1530s Dissolution, and can be seen in romantic grounds of Victorian house.

Beckermet St Bridget, Cumbria. 2 *crosses* of c. 1000, one inscribed, in yard of the old church.

Bedford. *St Peter de Merton,* Anglo-Saxon central tower of c. 1000 (originally W tower) with long-and-short work quoins, windows and doorway high up (originally access to wooden gallery). Fine Norman S doorway and bell-openings of tower. More Anglo-Saxon vestiges in present chancel (quoins outside, etc.).

Benington, Hertfordshire. Norman *keep's* low ruined walls (adorned with wild neo-Norman details) and gatehouse, in the garden of a Georgian house called The Lordship.

Bere Regis, Dorset. Grand *church* with nave arcades of c. 1160–80, the E parts Gothic. Massive tub font with carved intersecting arcades.

Berkhamsted, Hertfordshire. *Castle,* in Castle Street to riverside, shattered but impressive fragments of Thomas à Becket's flint walling of c. 1160 around large moated bailey, with earth motte in one corner.

Berkswell, West Midlands. Major and thrilling Norman *church,* with crypt (with mysterious octagon) and chancel, c. 1180, chancel arch and arcaded nave. Pevsner suggests octagon may be late Anglo-Saxon.

Bewcastle, Cumbria. In churchyard of St Cuthbert's, shaft of the famous *Bewcastle Cross* (23) of c. 700, said to be the finest of its date in Europe (with its sister-cross at Ruthwell (q.v.), over the Border). Nearly 15 ft high (its head vanished), it commemorates the Northumbrian King Alcfrith (died 670), and the Near East and Nordic sources detectable in its carving can be compared with the much later style of the Gosforth

Cross (q.v.) further S in Cumbria.

Billingham, Cleveland (Teesside). *Church,* tower and nave Anglo-Saxon of late 900s, though nave has Norman arcades inserted.

Binham, Norfolk. *Abbey church* of Norman Benedictine monastery. Nave of c. 1130 now parish church. Of the monastery, there are remains of Norman kitchen, refectory, etc.

Birkenhead, Merseyside. *St James's Priory,* founded c. 1150 (Benedictine), ruins in Priory Street among modern shipyards. Well-restored chapter house, c. 1190, with vaulting on corbels, and other late Norman fragments among later remains.

Birkin, North Yorkshire. SSW of Selby, small almost intact Norman *church* with nave, chancel and rib-vaulted apse, c. 1160. Fine carving (zigzag, beakhead and medallions) on doorways, windows and chancel arch. S aisle C14.

Birnie, Grampian Region. Unlikely (being so far north in the Lowlands, and just in surviving) almost intact little *church* (67) of the early Norman kind built in England soon after the Conquest. Nave and apse, simplest carving only, here probably of c. 1120–50.

Birsay, Mainland, Orkney. Earl Thorfinn of Orkney built small *cathedral* (124) here after pilgrimage to Rome, c. 1050. Largely ruined, but unusual circular chapels survive at E end of nave (perhaps c. 1050, more likely c. 1120) with other walling. *Brough of Birsay* (80) on the headland, remains of Earl Thorfinn's village of c. 1000–1100, one house with steam bathroom.

Bishop Auckland, County Durham. *Auckland Castle,* residence of bishops of Durham since C12. Present chapel (83) (interior) was the arcaded Great Hall built 1183 by Bishop Pudsey, though windows Gothicised and encrusted with memorials, etc.; other buildings later. (Not usually open to the public.) *South Church* of C13 contains reconstructed sculpted Anglian cross, c. 800.

Bishop's Cleeve, Gloucestershire. Splendid *church* (75) of c. 1160–90, nave and crossing with tower, rich carving, C13 chancel.

Bishops Waltham, Hampshire. Extensive ruins of the *Bishop's Palace* (83) started by Bishop Henry in c. 1130, enlarged extravagantly in c. 1170 (and again, c. 1500).

Bishopsteignton, Devon. W portal of *church* has rich carving of c. 1150, 2-order carved shafts and arches with zigzag, fish-scale, beakhead and flowers. On S side, tympanum with Mary and 3 kings, primitive. Font altered, rest of church Gothic.

Bishopstone, East Sussex. Much remains of Saxon *church* (27), c. 750 – S *porticus,* single-splayed window, inscribed sundial, long-and-short work quoins, carved coffin lid. Norman tower, chancel and aisle added. Zigzagged and Transitional arches.

Blewbury, Oxfordshire. Crossing and rib-vaulted chancel of *church* are c. 1190 (Gothicised E window) with waterleaf capitals, corbels and other late Norman and Transitional features (e.g. pointed arches).

Blisland, Cornwall. *Manor-house* (81, *149*), beside village green, has Norman wing on side lane, with doorway and 2 windows round-arched (from single stones) and masonry. Fine *church* has only Norman traces and tower.

Blyth, Nottinghamshire. *Priory church* (112, *148*), nave of c. 1090 only survives, grimly splendid early Norman architecture with strange little sculpted heads in capitals. Spaces resonant with unornamented post-Conquest feeling.

Boarhunt, Hampshire. Complete small Saxon *church,* c. 1060, nave and chancel, though windows all altered.

Bodmin, Cornwall. C15 parish church, *St Petroc,* has marvellous 5-columned sculpted font, c. 1190. Another like it is at Roche church, 7 miles SE.

Bolam, Northumberland. Church *tower,* c. 1050, with 3 triangular-headed windows. *Church* itself Norman and later.

Boothby Pagnell, Lincolnshire. Classic and well-preserved example of Norman country manor-house, built at the time when local lords started to move out of fortified dwellings: *Old Manor* (83, *84, 85*) is in grounds of early C19 Boothby Pagnell Hall (ask for permission to visit), just outside village. Originally moated, but no other defence when built in c. 1190–1200. Ground floor has vaulted undercroft (for storage, work and perhaps animals). Living quarters up

Blyth Priory church, Nottinghamshire. An example of early Norman sculpture, with detail of a primitively carved capital of the 1090s

external stone stairway, arriving in the hall (somewhat subdivided at present) and beyond that the solar or private chamber. Several original Norman windows, doorways and chimney at rear. *Church*, in village, nave arcades of c. 1140 and 1180 (as are tower and W door, with waterleaf capitals), chancel, c. 1300.

Borthwick, Lothian Region. 1½ miles SE of Gorebridge. *Church* has apse and S chancel wall, c. 1150; the rest Victorian restoration.

Bosham (pronounced Bozzam), West Sussex. Major Anglo-Saxon work in a largely later *church* (32). Lower tower, tower arch and splendid multiple roll-moulded chancel arch are those of Earl Godwin's church of c. 1040–50, built on site of a Romano-British church. S chapel in undercroft, c. 1200.

Bowes, North Yorkshire. *Castle* consists only of rectangular keep built 1171–90 for Henry II by one of his 'ingeniators' called Richard (see under Dover and Orford for castles by others).

Brabourne, Kent. Fine Norman sculpture in ornate *church* of c. 1180.

Bradford-on-Avon, Wiltshire. *St Laurence* (35, *35*), all of ashlar stone, quite small, one of the top rank of all late Anglo-Saxon churches. Lower walls probably of St Aldhelm's foundation of early 700s, upper parts, with their blank arcading and lesenes extended on to lower walls too, built in c. 950–1000, and double-splayed windows later. Tall, narrow and moving spaces and apertures. 1 transept destroyed, otherwise complete.

Bradwell-juxta-Mare, Essex. One of the rare largely preserved early Anglo-Saxon churches, reached by footpath (2 miles) signposted from Bradwell-on-Sea, N of Burnham-on-Crouch. A small building standing alone in a field, used as a barn until 1920s (cart entrances in walls now blocked), *St Peter* (17) was built in c. 654 by St Cedd, who went from Canterbury to be bishop of East Saxons. Nave only survives, but traces of vanished apse and 2 *porticus* in walls, which are of re-used Roman bricks. Simply and movingly restored.

Braunton, Devon. Fine *church*, itself C13 and C14, its handsome Norman tower with broach spire, positioned unusually beside nave.

Breamore, Hampshire. Lovely *church* (33, *33*), basically Anglo-Saxon, c. 1010, in lyrical setting. Transepts show Saxon

proportions – tall narrow form and steep roofline, with long-and-short work quoins. Much of church rebuilt, but retains large stone arch in crossing, inscribed by Saxon founder. S door has Saxon crucifixion group, defaced by Puritans.

Brechin, Tayside Region. In churchyard of C13 cathedral, tall *round tower* (40, *40*) (documentary evidence dates it between 990 and 1012) with sculpted doorway high above ground (see also under Abernethy). In cathedral, the sculpted *Aldbar Stone*, Northumbrian-style, of 880s.

Brecon, Powys. *Castle* remains, in grounds of present bishop's house, include scrap of shell-keep and small polygonal Ely Tower, c. 1180, on motte. *Cathedral* completely rebuilt from 1201.

Breedon-on-the-Hill, Leicestershire. *St Mary* (26, 27), on isolated hilltop above village and over huge quarry. Mercian monastery founded in c. 700, present church C13 and later, but about 30 pieces of Anglo-Saxon sculpture and carving embedded around inside walls

The grooved single-stone arch over the doorway and small single-stone arch windows of this house at Blisland, Cornwall, suggest a date nearer the Norman Conquest than any other known dwelling in England

and elsewhere. Carved frieze bands, lovely angel, Byzantine-style Virgin, etc., all of c. 700–800.

Bridekirk, Cumbria. *Dovenby Hall,* 1½ miles SW of village, has very early pele-tower (see under Mallerstang) with Norman window, c. 1200, though now almost embedded in the Georgian house (private).

Bridgend, Mid Glamorgan. *Castle,* called Newcastle, as is the part of Bridgend town on this side of the river. Mostly of c. 1190, polygonal curtain wall with 2 towers (like small rectangular keeps) set in walls. S tower has elaborate doorway with round and shallow segmented arches (billet motif and carved capitals), thought to be partly altered C16.

Bridgnorth, Shropshire. Of the *castle,* square keep of 1168–89 stands, though now leaning steeply over River Severn.

Brigstock, Northamptonshire. *Church,* lower part of tower Anglo-Saxon, c. 1000, on earlier base, with stairway turret like Brixworth (q.v.). Norman nave arcade, c. 1180.

Brinsop, Hereford and Worcester. C14

church, but contains excellent c. 1150–60 carved arches and tympanum showing St George. Of Shobdon (q.v.) school.

Bristol, Avon. *Cathedral* (100, *100,* 101, *150*), Gothic, but founded in c. 1140 as abbey of Augustinian Canons; their fine gatehouse (101) (top altered) and, down hill beyond, doorways of Dean's Lodging (101) survive, all ornate work of c. 1160–70. E range of cloister also exists, with simple doorways of c. 1145 and vestibule to chapter house (101, *101,* 102, *102*) – masterpiece of zigzag and blank-arcaded carved wall decoration, rib-vaulted, c. 1160–70. *St James,* Whitson Street, has Norman W front and wheel window. *Aisled Hall,* c. 1200, of a Norman house is now invisible behind modern panelling in Assize Court, Small Street, and should be rescued.

Britford, S of Salisbury, Wiltshire. *Church* (27) has notable *porticus* arch, reveals and soffits ornamented with 'ladder-rung' motif and vines with interlace (probably early 800s), together with tall nave of Anglo-Saxon proportions and another Saxon opening,

The rib-vaulted gatehouse of c. 1160–70 to the Augustinian Canons' precinct, Bristol cathedral. This is characteristic late Norman West Country work, with its spiral shafts with orders of developed multiple zigzag forming lozenge, intersecting arcade and interlace patterns

among other much later features.

Brixworth, Northamptonshire. *Church* (24, *24, 25,* 27, 38), grandest of all surviving early Anglo-Saxon churches. Built as monastic church, c. 680, by monks from Peterborough – 2-storey W porch, spacious aisled nave with clerestory, 3-arched opening to square chancel and apse, *porticus* N and S of chancel (*porticus* and nave aisles now vanished, and arcades blocked in as present N and S walls). Apse destroyed by Vikings and rebuilt C10, when W porch was built upwards to become present tower and W projecting stairway turret added (tower's spire, battlements and many windows are post-Norman, S doorway Norman).

Broadstairs, Kent. Like at Margate (q.v.), *St Peter* has long Norman nave. Chancel later.

Brompton-in-Allertonshire, North Yorkshire. *Church* has 2 crosses of 900s, shaft of 800s, several Anglo-Norse hogback tombs with rearing bears, N arcade of c. 1190, waterleaf and octagonal abaci; the rest C19.

Bronllys, Powys. *Castle,* motte-and-bailey earthworks of c. 1100, with fine well-preserved circular keep (55) of c. 1200 on the motte. 4 storeys – basement, guardroom, hall (fireplace and 2 windows) and solar chamber, with stairs in walls. Similarities to Conisbrough (q.v.).

Brough, Cumbria. 3 walls of square keep, c. 1180, survive at this hilltop *castle,* also some early Norman herringbone masonry in curtain wall.

Brougham, Cumbria. *Castle,* by river outside town and attractive to visit. Rectangular keep (48), c. 1180, stands full height (though window surrounds destroyed), crowded in by later buildings and walls – the whole rescued by Lady Anne Clifford in 1660, as were castles at Appleby (q.v.), Brough (q.v.), Pendragon at Mallerstang (q.v.), Skipton, etc.

Broughton, Humberside. *Church* (38, *38*) has late Anglo-Saxon tower, c. 1000, made imposing by its massive masonry, plus herringbone, and projecting stair turret added before 1066. Broad tower arch inside – tower interior may have provided nave. Present nave and chancel C13 and C14. Interlace carved stone panel, C11, in a chapel.

Buckland, Oxfordshire. *Church,* tall roll-moulded S doorway, c. 1110, and

wide Norman nave; the rest Gothic.

Buildwas, Shropshire. *Abbey,* founded 1135 for French monks who became Cistercian in 1147, but buildings seem to date from 1160 onwards. Ruins of church, chapter house, etc., plus early C13 Gothic infirmary.

Buncton, West Sussex. Notably preserved tall nave, c. 1090, with minute windows, in small rustic *church* (61) – but with inexplicable sophisticatedly carved external arches, c. 1160, in N wall.

Bungay, Suffolk. *Castle,* its square keep with massive forebuilding, though both stand only to 1st-floor level. Built in c. 1140 by Roger Bigod, Norman magnate of East Anglia, and captured from rebellious Bigods in 1174 by Henry II, whose undermining can still be seen in one corner (see under Orford).

Burpham, West Sussex. Fine Norman *church,* nave partly of c. 1100, S transept richly ornate, c. 1160, chancel, c. 1180. Some later windows. Well restored by T. G. Jackson, 1869.

Burton Agnes, Humberside. Rare surviving Norman manor-house, c. 1170 (see Chapter 4), the *Old Manor* (82) in grounds of Burton Agnes Hall. Exterior rebuilt in brick, but inside is the stone hall (some later alterations) on upper floor, chimney and stone spiral stairs, rib-vaulted undercroft beneath.

Bury St Edmunds, Suffolk. Extensive fragments off modern town-centre square of great Benedictine abbey, 1081–1140, on site of earlier monastery marking martyrdom of King Edmund by the Danes, 869. *Abbey church* (destroyed after Dissolution in 1530s), no more than nightmarish lumps of flint and cement showing outlines, now in public park. *Monastic buildings,* whose chief early monument is the Norman gatehouse (97, *99*), major building of 1120–48, its tall fort-like mass relieved by enriched portal, intersecting arcading, zigzag carving, etc. Other fragments (entrance to destroyed treasury and various scraps of wall) lie among present houses in precinct (also Great Gate, C14, St James Cathedral, C16). *Moyses Hall* (88), in Cornhill (market place), 2-storey Norman stone house, c. 1180, with round arches and windows, hall and solar (private chamber) on upper level. Some alterations. (Open to the public.)

Byland Abbey, North Yorkshire. (75,

103). Cistercian abbey, founded 1177. Plan and N side of church survive as spectacular ruin of c. 1180–1200, with E ambulatory and chapels (contrary to earlier Cistercian plans, to St Bernard's simple rules; see under Fountains, Rievaulx and Chapter 5), pointed arches, waterleaf capitals, corbels, etc., aisled transepts. Cloister, chapter house and refectory ruins largely Norman Transitional, c. 1200; the rest C13, etc.

Caldey Island, off coast of Dyfed. By boat from Tenby. Modern *monastery* preserves evocative ruins of Norman Benedictine monastic buildings, tower and chapel, on site of Celtic foundation (where St Samson, late patron saint of Brittany, was abbot in c. 550).

Cambridge. *St Bene't's Church*, St Bene't Street, Anglo-Saxon tower and tower arch, and some walling of nave corners and chancel S side, all of c. 1040; the rest Gothic. *St Mary Magdalene*, Newmarket Road, Barnwell (suburb), complete small Norman church (built as chapel for leper hospital), nave and chancel only, all of c. 1150, with zigzag enrichment, well restored by G. G. Scott, 1867. *Holy Sepulchre* (77), Bridge Street, famous round church (see also under London, Northampton and Orphir), built by the 'Fraternity of the Holy Sepulchre' on the model of the Holy Sepulchre Church, Jerusalem, in c. 1130: circular nave with short round piers and gallery, sculptural enrichment well blended with the forceful forms, ribbed dome, rib-vaulted ambulatory around. Restored by Salvin, 1841, who also added Gothic oblong chancel. *Castle*, Castle Street, only earthwork motte of Conqueror's castle of c. 1068 remains. *Jesus College* contains quite extensive remains of St Radegond's Benedictine nunnery, founded c. 1130, but subsequent rebuildings make it unclear whether anything is earlier than chapter house of c. 1220. *'School of Pythagoras'* (87) (now property of St John's College), behind terrace of brick cottages of C18, Nos. 20–30 Northampton Street. Probably private house, c. 1190, stone and rubble construction, undercroft (once vaulted) and hall above, with fireplace and 2 2-light windows of slightly later date, as is solar and western end of house (1373). Staircase and bay window, 1967.

Canford Magna, Dorset. Fascinating *church*, with chancel of c. 1000 –

originally the Anglo-Saxon nave (note 2 *porticus*). Norman tower, N and S doorways and arcaded nave (without piers) of c. 1170, and fine Victorian W end in Transitional style (by D. Brandon, 1876).

Canterbury, Kent. Evocative series of 4 early Anglo-Saxon (Jutish?) churches along typically prehistoric and pre-Christian E–W alignment, with 2 standing stones at W end of series and large mound nearby, mostly now in enclosed ruins of *St Augustine's Priory* (14) (open to the public) on St Martin's Hill to the E outside city walls. *St Martin's Church* (13, *14*, 15, *16*, 65) (furthest E of series) is still in use, and Roman brickwork wall on N of chancel, with long flat-topped *porticus* entry blocked (visible inside and out), is probably part of Queen Bertha's church (late Roman?) already there when St Augustine arrived from Rome in 597. Other doorway nearby, and walls of nave, probably of early 600s, as are buttresses outside; the rest is later restoration from ruined state. Further W, in E–W succession within enclosed priory area, are low ruins of: *St Pancras* (15, *16*), 17), ruined church of 600s (built of Roman bricks) but enough walls remain to evoke shape, nave, apsed chancel, 3 *porticus* (the W one largely preserved); *St Mary* (15), foundations only of King Edbald's church of c. 620 (for royal burials) among ruins of later easterly crypt of the Norman abbey built over all the rest of the Anglo-Saxon churches to W of this; *St Peter and St Paul* (14, *16*, 17), Augustine's main church (Bede says 'of becoming splendour'), built 598–613, outline of nave 27 ft wide visible. 2 *porticus*, N and S (of Roman bricks) intended for major burials, can be seen. S *porticus* contained 3 early archbishops, with St Augustine himself buried by altar against E wall; N *porticus* contained King Aethelbert and Queen Bertha. Later Anglo-Saxon additions around this church included a *narthex* to the W (more burials), a chamber by N *porticus*, a 2nd westerly *narthex* and vestibule beyond – so that it became a mysterious series of spaces around inner sanctum. (Between St Mary and St Peter and St Paul, the *Rotunda* of Abbot Wulfric – crypt foundations visible of this later Anglo-Saxon unique structure of c. 1050–60.) All this swept away above ground level when 1st Norman abbot built large abbey, 1073–91. Pier and wall foundations of Norman *abbey church* visible only, except crypt remains and part of 1 aisle wall built into palace for Henry VIII, who destroyed almost the whole abbey after Dissolution of the Monasteries in 1537. His palace too now in ruins, though parts of it and monastic dwellings now in Victorian monastic college abutting site. *Cathedral* (10, 75, 95, 126, 127, *127*). Augustine reconsecrated a Roman church in the city in 602, which was enlarged in c. 950 and entirely replaced by Archbishop Lanfranc's Norman cathedral (and monastery) started in 1070, itself replaced (nave only in 1391–1405) by Anselm's choir in 1096–1130 (though Lanfranc's crypt and various chapels survive); this choir gutted by fire in 1174 and its interior rebuilt and enlarged on a swelling plan in *avant-garde* style of 1175–84 (for pilgrims to the new 1170 martyr St Thomas à Becket's relics) in earliest pointed-arch Gothic manner from France. Trinity Chapel at E and its crypt and corona part of this Transitional work (c. 1180–4), pointed and round arches but still with Norman zigzag. Wall-paintings of c. 1150 in crypt and St Anselm's Chapel (96). *Cathedral monastic buildings* (95, 97), extensive Norman work: Lanfranc's *dormitory undercroft* (95), c. 1080 and c. 1110, with very early zigzag, etc. (now partly under modern library) and NE corner of 1st-floor *dormitory* (95) itself. Arcaded wall of *infirmary* (95), c. 1120. *Treasury* (96, 96) building, with rich ornament, c. 1150. *Lavatorium Tower* (96), fine vaulting beneath, c. 1150. *Infirmary Cloister* (95, 96), 2 arcaded sides only, c. 1150 and c. 1190. *Court Gatehouse* (96) and *North Hall* (96, 97, *98*) (on far side of the Green Court), built c. 1160 to accommodate important pilgrims (famous ornate stone staircase entrance to Hall, interior rebuilt). Other Norman, etc., buildings: *St Mildred*, Church Lane, has S nave wall of Anglo-Saxon church, interior later. *St Stephen*, Hackington, nave and transepts of c. 1110, rest altered. *Castle*, Castle Street and Ring Road, lower parts of large keep of c. 1100. *Eastbridge Hospital* (*91*, 92), St Peter's Street, later exterior, but inside there is vaulted undercroft, upper aisled hall and chapel of hostel, dedicated to St

Thomas à Becket, of c. 1180, with lovely contemporary wall-painting of Christ in *vesica pisces* in hall.

Cardiff, South Glamorgan. *Castle* (45), largely a Victorian masterpiece, but Norman motte and shell-keep, c. 1200, preserved. *Llandaff Cathedral* (125), in western suburbs of city, Norman cathedral started in c. 1120 (W and S doorways and chancel arch at E survive), nave rebuilt from c. 1170 onwards, the whole in ruins after Dissolution of Monasteries in 1537, restored and reconstructed (especially by John Prichard, 1850–70) and later intrusions added. Cross of 900s in S chancel aisle.

Cardinham, Cornwall. Fine interlace, etc., carved *cross* (*23*) by church entrance perhaps of 800s. Latin-inscribed *stone* in churchyard.

Carisbrooke, Isle of Wight. *Castle* (45), shell-keep and curtain wall of c. 1160, plus interior of C12 Great Hall inside later building. *Church*, early Norman, c. 1100, with nave arcade of 1190s.

Carlisle, Cumbria. *Cathedral*, started as Augustinian abbey church, c. 1130 (though founded by Henry I, 1102), but cathedral from 1133. Crossing and transepts of 1130–60 survive; the rest rebuilt C13 and C19. *Castle*, the key W defence of the border against Scotland. Henry II's rectangular keep (48), c. 1160, with triangular inner bailey, plus later works, is still there.

Carlton-in-Lindrick, Nottinghamshire. Lower part of church tower is of c. 1000, upper part herringbone masonry, c. 1050 (pinnacles and buttresses C14). *Church* itself a major Norman piece, though nave and chancel walls may be pre-Conquest (and 2 windows), tower arch pre-1100, arcades of c. 1170–90, as are chancel arch, chapels and front. E window and roofs Gothic.

Cartmel, Cumbria. No remains of Augustinian domestic buildings, founded 1188, but *priory church* of c. 1190–1220 is splendidly complete. Transitional chancel, N door, transepts and nave built in that order and showing move into Early English Gothic in upper parts.

Cassington, Oxfordshire. *Church*, c. 1120, aisleless nave, lower part of tower, fine corbel-table. Some later alterations.

Castle Acre, Norfolk. *Castle*, very grand stone shell-keep, c. 1190, on earlier motte and big bailey earthworks. *Priory*

church (94) (Cluniac), c. 1130, in ruins. Ornate W front and 1 bay of zigzagged interior still stand. Outline of foundations visible, and fragments of Norman monastery buildings (kitchen, infirmary and gateway). *Parish church*, post-Norman.

Castle Hedingham, Essex. *Castle*, magnificent keep built in c. 1130 by Earl of Oxford on earlier motte. Finely preserved, with big hall on 2nd floor, zigzagged fireplace and windows. *Church*, Tudor outside, but complete and excellent building of c. 1160 within, and ornate chancel, c. 1190.

Castle Rising, Norfolk. *Castle* (48), splendid Norman hall-keep among vast earthworks and with deep moat. Gatehouse, c. 1160, quite simple. Keep also of c. 1160, but with much decorative carving, especially on forebuilding entrance. Great Hall within and other Norman features including chapel. *Church*, fine W front and interior, c. 1160, with various later alterations.

Castle Roy, near Nethybridge, Highland Region. (57.) Early stone castle for Scotland, c. 1200, simple quadrangular curtain wall around courtyard, with some fragments of living quarters within.

Castle Sween, by Loch Sween, Strathclyde Region. (57, 59, *59*.) Visible from lochside main road, on hillock by the water. Massive quadrangular shell-keep, c. 1200, large round-topped entrance arch and flat Norman-type buttresses, originally with timber buildings inside (rear wing C13). Built by Sweyn, Celtic-Norse piratical prince of Knapdale, and earliest ambitious castle to survive in Scotland.

Castor, Cambridgeshire. Spectacular Norman *church* of 1124 (dedication stone in chancel), fine arcaded crossing tower over cruciform plan. At this date, only just too early for zigzag carving (see under Durham). Chancel and some alterations C14.

Chaldon, Surrey. Tiny flint *church* of c. 1180, with huge primitive wall-painting of Heaven and Hell, c. 1200, all over W internal wall.

Chaluim Chille (pronounced approximately Calum Kill), Skye, Inner Hebrides. Sometimes called Annait (called so by Dr Johnson after an Egyptian god), Chaluim Chille means Columba's place. Remains of a subsidiary *monastery* (13) from Iona

include small chapel, 2 monks' cells, cashel or wall enclosure, and causeway from its promontory position to dry land. Loch Chaluim Chille lies W of B886, partly dried out now, exposing the site.

Chapel Finian, Dumfries and Galloway Region. In a remote place, overlooking the sea, 6 miles N of Port William near A747. Oval walled enclosure, well and low walls (buttressed) of chapel, c. 1000.

Chapel in the Rocks, Dumfries and Galloway Region. In the cliff overlooking Luce Bay, S of Kirkmadrine on the very tip of the Mull of Galloway, near the lighthouse. Remains of chapel using a cave as its chancel and building out a nave of drystone slates 11 ft long by 9 ft wide. Associated with St Modan, but of unknown Dark Ages date.

Charleston Manor, East Sussex. See under Westdean.

Chatham, Kent. *Chapel* of St Bartholomew's Hospital, High Street, c. 1130, restored by G. G. Scott, C19.

Checkendon, Oxfordshire. Little *church*, aisleless nave, chancel and apse with ornate arches, though only 1 Norman window survives in apse.

Chepstow, Gwent. Major *castle*, mostly post-Norman, but lower parts of the (now floorless and roofless) keep were the 1st-floor hall of the early Norman castle (started c. 1070 in stone, but hall probably a bit later) and its doorway and architectural details are still visible on walls inside. *Church*, in town square, has Norman tower (top altered) and nave (much altered).

Chester. *Cathedral*, started as Benedictine abbey church in c. 1100 (became cathedral in 1540), N transept and 2 fragments in choir, c. 1100–20. St Anselm's Chapel, NW tower, cloister S wall and undercroft, c. 1120, abbot's passage, c. 1150, crossing and nave, Gothic, C14 and C15. *St John the Baptist*, briefly the cathedral from 1175 to 1195, appears largely Victorian but has nave, crossing and 1 bay of chancel, c. 1180. *Castle*, beside the river, with fragments of so-called Caesar's Tower (and c. 1200 chapel in it) among Greek Revival masterpiece of 1785–1822. *Walls*, S and W sections (beside Castle Drive and City Walls Road, for example) include C12 first medieval additions to ancient Roman wall, but not the most impressive stretches (which are C13 with later additions).

Chichester, West Sussex. *Cathedral* (100) of great charm, not especially large but impressively sited. Built mostly in c. 1090–1184 (choir, nave and transepts basically survive), but after 1187 fire much rebuilt, from 1190 onwards (adding clerestory and decoration, etc.). E end and upper levels of church again altered C14, spire C15. 2 splendid sculpted panels (Lazarus and Christ), c. 1140, in choir aisle. *Precinct* (for canons, since cathedral never monastic), undercroft of the Vicars' Hall now coffee-house. In Canons' Lane, a Norman doorway.

Chickney, Essex. Small *church* with Saxon nave and windows, C11.

Chilham, Kent. *Castle* (52), impressive tall octagonal keep on motte built by Henry II, 1171 (the master 'ingeniator', or mason, was Ralph, who also built Dover Castle (q.v.) with another mason called Mauricius), with projecting turrets for stairs and garderobes, and forebuilding (which originally took in an undefended stone Hall of c. 1100, now gone).

Chobham, Surrey. *Church,* late Norman arcade and chapel, c. 1180, added to early Norman nave. Chancel Victorian.

Chollerton, Northumberland. *Church,* unusual arcaded nave of c. 1140 with re-used Roman columns.

Cholsey, Oxfordshire. *Church,* bottom of crossing tower late Anglo-Saxon, c. 1050. Nave and transepts, c. 1160 (originally with apsed chancels), but Norman chancel rebuilt.

Christchurch, Hampshire. *Priory church,* important Augustinian centre even before it became a priory in 1150. Crypts tunnel-vaulted, c. 1095, transepts and crossing, c. 1110, unusual N transept frontage, c. 1130. *Castle,* 2 walls of Norman keep, c. 1170, stand on the motte, but special interest is the remains of 2-storey Hall (83) of c. 1180.

Claverley, Shropshire. *Church,* nave, N aisle and lower part of tower early and late Norman. N side of nave has long strip wall-painting, c. 1200, of a battle.

Clayton, East Sussex. *Church,* Saxon chancel arch, c. 1040, and extraordinary wall-paintings, c. 1150–80.

Climping, West Sussex. *Church,* mostly C13, but unusual carving and zigzag, c. 1180, over lower tower windows and doorway.

Clitheroe, Lancashire. *Castle,* small 3-storey keep on rock overlooking town.

Clun, Shropshire. *Church* with unusual chunky tower, the interior largely Norman too, of various stages, though much restored by G. E. Street, 1877. *Castle* stands high above river across the bridge from church, with well-preserved ruined keep, plus C13 towers.

Colchester, Essex. *Castle* (47), massive 2-storey hall-keep (upper levels intended but never completed) built in c. 1080 for William I's defences against Norse invasion. Apsed projecting chapel (see under White Tower, London). Original stone facing vanished, leaving flint core. *St Botolph's Priory* church, in ruins, the Augustinian Canons' powerful nave, c. 1090, with portals and towers, c. 1160. *Holy Trinity,* Trinity Street, Victorian church with Saxon W tower, c. 1020–40, and triangular-headed doorway.

Coldingham, Borders Region. *Priory church* of small Benedictine monastery, long chancel of c. 1200 survives.

Colerne, Wiltshire. Viking-style shaft of cross of 800s with dragons in *church,* which has Transitional nave arcades of c. 1200, round piers with rare octagonal abaci and single-stepped pointed arches on 1 side, chamfered arches and even some Early English-type stiff-leaf on other.

Coln Rogers, Gloucestershire. Endearing *church,* fabric of nave and chancel Anglo-Saxon, perhaps 1030 judging by surviving chancel arch, door and window.

Colyton, Devon. *Church* has crossing (tower above it later), Transitional with pointed arches, c. 1180–90, but is most notable for parts of a cross's shaft, c. 1000, with animals and interlace.

Compton, Surrey. Major Norman *church,* notable chancel, c. 1180, 2-storeyed (the lower arched and vaulted), both storeys open to fine earlier Norman nave under main chancel arch. Good carving throughout.

Compton Martin, Somerset. This major *church* (69) has nave with rare Durham-type spiralling incised drum-piers, c. 1120–30, and rib-vaulted chancel perhaps a little earlier.

Conisbrough, South Yorkshire. The late Norman nobleman's *castle* (52, 53, 54, 55, 55) *par excellence,* built overlooking valley by Hameline

Plantagenet (Henry II's half-brother). Round keep, c. 1180, with extraordinary powerful buttresses around it (containing chapel and various other chambers), fine stonework, no floors inside but fireplaces, windows, etc. Inner bailey curtain wall, etc., c. 1200. *Church*, on another nearby hill, largely Norman, c. 1175.

Copford, Essex. Notable Norman *church* (75), nave, chancel and apse with rare wall-paintings of perhaps c. 1150–80 in apse, nave, chancel arch, etc.

Corbridge, Northumberland. Of Anglo-Saxon (Northumbrian kingdom) *church* (20) of c. 780, lower part of tower (at first 2-storey porch) and parts of nave walls can be seen. Upper tower late Anglo-Saxon, c. 1030. Also some Norman features, e.g. S doorway, but rest C13, etc. Churches near Corbridge include those at *Bywell*, tower C8 below, C10 or C11 above, and *Ovingham*, lower tower C10.

Corfe, Dorset. Mighty,devastated *castle* on hillock in strategic gap in hills. William I built a (vanished) castle here; Henry I the part-surviving present high keep (48), c. 1110–20, with bailey wall; John strengthened these walls and added the hall (Gloriette), in fragments E of keep, in 1201–4, the outer walls, 1235–80. Ruined by O. Cromwell *et al.* in 1640s.

Corley, Warwickshire. Largely Norman *church* with S doorway, nave and chancel arch, c. 1110, arcade, c. 1170, chancel C13.

Cossans, Tayside Region. St Orland's *slab cross*, c. 700?

Cropthorne, Hereford and Worcester. Fine Mercian *cross's head*, with birds and animals, interlace and key-pattern, Anglo-Saxon of c. 850, in partly Norman church.

Crowland, Lincolnshire. *Croyland Abbey* at Crowland. No work of St Guthlac's monastery of c. 980 survives, nor of Norman Benedictine monks' dwellings. But there are remnants of S aisle façade and other parts, c. 1114–90, among later work, of the abbey church.

Culbone, Somerset. Tiny isolated *church*, W of Porlock and Minehead, basically Norman, though most features altered (reredos and memorial by C. F. A. Voysey), but moving to visit.

Cury, Cornwall. *Church* has ornate S doorway, c. 1150.

Dacre, Cumbria. Partly Norman *St Andrew*, 2 crosses of c. 900 and c. 950 in churchyard.

Dalmeny, Lothian Region. With Leuchars (q.v.) the finest Norman Romanesque *church* (77) in Scotland. W tower (restored), nave, chancel and apse, c. 1150–60. Rich S doorway, 2-order sculpted arches and interlaced arcading plus corbel-table above. Inside, zigzagged chancel and apse arches, both these spaces rib-vaulted. (See under Tyninghame for ruins of similar church.)

Davington, Kent. Ruins of *nunnery* include nave and W front of c. 1160.

Deeping St James, Lincolnshire. Nave of Benedictine monks' *church* survives, with long S arcade, c. 1190, and font.

Deerhurst, Gloucestershire. *St Mary's* priory church (27, *30*, 31, *31*), perhaps the loveliest and most magical of all Anglo-Saxon churches. Complex history: tall white nave of 700s (arcades inserted C13) with W porch (now lower part of tower) and chancel with *porticus* (now E side-chapels). Altered in 800s (more *porticus* added, now aisles) and again in c. 1020, when present tower built (changed openings from tower into nave visible on W wall) and apsed chancel rebuilt (chancel arch visible in E wall, apse lies in ruins beyond it). *Earl Odda's Chapel* lies a short walk further along lane approaching church, on the left. Simple building of 1053–6, with typical Anglo-Saxon tall narrow proportions. Completely preserved, but now at one end of a farmhouse.

Deerness, Mainland, Orkney. On cape called Brough of Deerness lie ruins of extensive Celtic-Norse *monastery* (13) (probably C8–11) with chapel and some 20 monks' cells inside cashel or wall enclosure.

Devizes, Wiltshire. *St John*, major church of 1100s within castle's bailey, has Norman tower and crossing, corbel-table, magnificent chancel with rib-vaulting and zigzagged blank arcading, pointed arches in crossing perhaps as early as 1160. *St Mary*, original town church, has corbel-table, zigzag on porch and another ornate rib-vaulted chancel.

Dewsbury, West Yorkshire. Victorianised main church of *All Saints* contains 3 parts of fine Anglian cross, c. 820, and other sculpture.

Diddlebury, Shropshire. *Church* has Anglo-Saxon nave with window and door, N wall all herringbone masonry, c. 1060. *Heath Chapel*, alone in fields 1 mile E of Diddlebury, perfectly preserved little Norman church, nave and square-ended chancel, c. 1130.

Dinas Emrys, Gwynedd. Beside A498 7 miles NW of Portmadoc, primarily an evocative Dark Ages earthworks site on hilltop (the Emrys of the name is Merlin), but on top the remains of a Norman *keep*.

Dolbadarn, Gwynedd. Outside Llanberis in Snowdonia, Welsh *castle* with curtain wall of late 1100s around rock peak, then the round keep, added in c. 1200 (or a little later) and used by Llywelyn the Great.

Dolton, Devon. Victorian *church* has font formed from notable interlaced and figure-sculpted Anglo-Saxon cross's shaft.

Dolwyddelan, Gwynedd. Above A496 from Betws-y-coed to Blaenau Ffestiniog. Welsh rectangular *keep* (57, *58*) of c. 1190 on hilltop (birthplace of Llywelyn the Great in 1200), with its upper storey and other buildings added later by the English.

Dorchester, Oxfordshire. *Abbey*, church on site granted by King of Wessex to St Birinus for a monastery in 634. Completely rebuilt, c. 1180, on cruciform plan without aisles or arcades, though only fragments of Norman features have survived later rebuildings.

Dover, Kent. *St Mary-in-Castro* (33), within castle outer wall, beside Roman lighthouse. Major Saxon church, the basic fabric and arches of the cross-planned Anglo-Saxon of c. 1000 still impressive, despite deplorable decoration after restoration in 1860 by G. G. Scott. *Castle* (56, *57*), the major Norman castle of England, London apart. Probably wooden structure till 1168 when Henry II decided to guard the Channel. Masons ('ingeniators') were Ralph and Mauricius. Huge tower keep (most windows now altered) was completed 1184, with its inner curtain wall and 11 turrets – one of the first such in Europe (see under Chilham and Orford for others of Henry's experiments). Tremendous forebuilding provides entrance and chapel above for keep, both with ornate zigzag. 2 main halls, both 2-storeyed. Inner curtain wall has lost original battlements but retains original rectangular towers with arrow-slits outwards and along walls. Outer curtain wall started by Henry, but mostly by King John in 1204–15. *St James*, Castle Hill Road, Norman but in bombed ruins. *St Mary*, Cannon Street, tower and arcaded nave, c. 1110. *St Martin's Priory*, now part of Dover College, Effingham Crescent. Chapel was *Guest Hall* of c. 1190 (altered). *Refectory* is 100 ft long, major survival of c. 1140 architecture, big round-arched windows and blank arcades along all walls inside.

Dryburgh Abbey, near St Boswells, Borders Region. (102, *103*.) In solitary position N of St Boswells, signposted up side-road from B6404, the poetic ruins of a Premonstratensian Canons' (see Chapter 5) abbey founded in c. 1150 from Alnwick, Northumberland, by invitation of David I or his constable. W front of church and fine cloister buildings, with 3-order round-arched doorways, and barrel-vaulted chapter house are of c. 1150–90, as are a few other features among later remnants.

Dumfries, Dumfries and Galloway Region. Museum in the *Old Observatory* has rich collection of carved stone crosses and a carved Northumbrian pillar (from Ruthwell), gathered from several places in SW Scotland.

Dunblane, Central Region. David I founded the *cathedral*, c. 1130, and tall square tower with 2-light belfry openings, primitive in style, survives with rebuilt C13 church.

Dunfermline, Fife Region. The great *abbey church* (97, 115, *118*, 124) of Scotland (and burial place of 11 kings and queens). Benedictine monastery founded by the notable Queen Margaret, c. 1070. David I brought Abbot Geoffrey from Canterbury in 1128, who built church for dedication in 1150. Doorways and splendid nave survive, the foremost Romanesque monument N of Durham. Arcades of monumental drum-piers, some drums incised with large zigzag or spiral patterns in Durham style, roll-mouldings and battlement motif on arches, gallery and clerestory above punched boldly through wall but with ornamented inner arches, nave flat-roofed but aisles rib-vaulted. (Visible through floor-grilles, foundations of early Celtic chapel and Queen Margaret's small apsed church, beneath nave.) Choir and crossing, ruined, were rebuilt to new design in 1818, serving as parish church and containing Robert the Bruce's tomb (Victorian cover). *Monastic buildings*, extensive C14, little Norman. *Queen Margaret's shrine*, E of church, simple with chapel foundations. *King Malcolm's Tower*, W of abbey 100 yards, in a park (follow signs up to cragtop keep ruins), probably C12 or earlier original stronghold, ineptly restored.

Dunham Magna, Norfolk. Major Anglo-Danish *church*, c. 1040, nave with good arcading and decoration, square tower. Chancel rebuilt.

Dunning, Tayside Region. *Church* has powerful Norman-style tower, c. 1150.

Dunstable, Bedfordshire. Major *church* survives of St Peter's Priory for Augustinian Canons, founded 1131 by Henry I. W front with splendid 4-order doorway, c. 1190 (carved capitals and medallions), and enriched intersecting blank arcading - upper frontage c. 1220. Spacious nave c. 1150 below, c. 1180-90 in higher levels. Timber roof and E parts of church are post-Norman. *Priory domestic building*, little remains except rib-vaulted undercroft of c. 1200 (now in private house called The Priory in the High Street) and Gothic gatehouse.

Durham. *Cathedral* (8, 68, 95, 114, 115, *115, 116, 117, 159*), the great masterpiece (with Norwich) of the Norman cathedrals. The miraculously uncorrupt body of St Cuthbert was brought here by monks in 995 to save it from the Danes' destruction of Lindisfarne (q.v.) and the 'White Church' was built by 1017. Rebuilt by Normans from 1093 onwards as major religious centre for the North. Chancel (or choir), 1093-c. 1104 (with apse later replaced by surviving lovely Gothic E end), N transept by c. 1110, crossing with S transept (and E end of nave) started c. 1105, S transept vaulted by c. 1115?, nave (with 1st zigzag vaulting and incised drum-piers) completed by Bishop Flambard with vaulting, W towers apparently all by 1133, and western Galilee Chapel, c. 1170 (for Venerable Bede's bones, stolen from Jarrow by a Durham monk). Central tower, C15, and E end, C13, only are post-Norman, as are most of extensive monastic buildings on S side. *Castle*, its chapel of c. 1090, while Bishop Pudsey built the obviously Norman walls (visible among the rest from the riverside), lower part of gatehouse, hall and Norman

Gallery, c. 1160; the rest of later periods. *Bridges.* It has been claimed that some parts of Framwellgate Bridge (1128 by outrageous venial Bishop Flambard) and Elvet Bridge (1160) on the river are still of Norman masonry.

Dymock, Gloucestershire. *Church* of c. 1100 with fine blank arcading and chancel arch, but famous for its S doorway and chancel arch of c. 1130-40, with zigzag arches, tympanum with Tree of Life and figure sculpture in capitals. Believed that same master-craftsman worked at Pauntley (q.v.) and Kempley (q.v.) and perhaps at Bridstow, Peterstow and Rockford in what is now Hereford and Worcester.

Dynevor, Dyfed. Hilltop dramatic *castle* above A40 along Vale of Tywi from Llandeilo. Big round late Norman keep (55) was the stronghold of Rhys family, rulers of most of S Wales. Curtain wall later.

Earls Barton, Northamptonshire. *Church* (*37, 38*), with famous late Anglo-Saxon tower, c. 1020, decorated with elaborate patterns of lesenes (stone pilaster-strips) set in cement. Norman chancel, c. 1140-50, with zigzagged arcading.

Eassie, Tayside Region. Slab *cross*, c. 700?, in the old churchyard.

East Barnet, Hertfordshire. Tiny early Norman *church*, with little windows in massive wall of nave; the rest Victorian.

East Meon, Hampshire. Major Norman *church* (76) of c. 1150, cruciform plan, doorway and crossing tower enriched with zigzag. Interior largely Norman with early C13 additions. One of the famous black Tournai marble fonts of c. 1140, with figure sculpture of Adam and Eve scenes.

Eastbourne, East Sussex. *St Mary*, Church Street, in the old town. Interesting Transitional nave and chancel arch, c. 1200 (some arches pointed, with 3-dimensional zigzag and stiff-leaf capitals); the rest later.

Easthorpe, Essex. Pretty little Norman *church*, attractively sited. Apse removed C13.

Edgeworth, Gloucestershire. *Church* has Anglo-Saxon N door and masonry, Norman chancel and bad Victorian restoration.

Edinburgh, Lothian Region. Of the Anglo-Norman Romanesque churches built under the Normanised and feudalising King David I (reigned 1124–53), several survive in villages around Edinburgh (see map). In modern Edinburgh, *Duddingston church*, in SE suburb beyond Arthur's Seat, is basically Norman. In the *castle*, the so-called Queen Margaret's Chapel (*77*) is a charming small church, with aisleless nave, chancel arch and apsed chancel, of c. 1180.

Edlingham, Northumberland. Small Norman *church*, chancel arch and porch (rare C12 feature and, just as rarely, tunnel-vaulted), c. 1100, while nave arcade is of c. 1180 and tower a little later.

Edstaston, Shropshire. Superb *church*, nave and chancel, corbel-tables complete, 3 splendid ornate doorways with inventive geometrical motifs plus lozenge and zigzag, all c. 1180.

Egilsay, Orkney. *St Magnus* (see under Kirkwall), design in the Irish tradition, barrel-vaulted chancel and round tower. Generally dated c. 1110, but might be much earlier.

Egremont, Cumbria. *Castle* has early Norman herringbone walling and gatehouse with unusual domed rib-vaulting of c. 1140 inside.

Eilach-an-Naoimh, Inner Hebrides.

Extraordinary and moving remains of walls of St Columba's 2nd *monastery* (13), on one of the tiny Garvelloch Islands at mouth of Firth of Lorne and S of Iona. Remains (of perhaps c. 700–c. 900) are of 3 round monks' cells, chapel with simple door and window, and grave enclosed by round wall. Very difficult to reach, but boats can sometimes be hired at Ardfern on the mainland or Easdale on Seil.

Elkstone, Gloucestershire. Outstanding Norman *church* (*160*), much carving of c. 1170 on corbel-table and S door Christ tympanum (less skilled), nave and chancel, including beakhead (some human heads here), zigzag and battlement motifs, pellets and zodiac animals.

Elsdon, Northumberland. NE of village, good example of c. 1066 motte-and-bailey *castle*, earthwork mound and banks only – no timber buildings survive, of course, and no stone ones were ever there (see Chapter 2).

Elstow, Bedfordshire. *Church* was that of Benedictine nunnery founded late C11. 3 bays of austere nave of c. 1100; other impressive buildings post-Norman. Carved stone panel of c. 1150 (Christ in *vesica* frame) over N doorway. Some monastic remains near church.

Durham cathedral. Late Norman ornament in the western Galilee Chapel of c. 1170

The chancel of Elkstone church, Gloucestershire (c. 1170), one of many well-preserved late Norman parish churches in western England

Ely, Cambridgeshire. *Cathedral* (27, 95, 122, 123), largely Norman and especially lovely. Monastery founded by St Aethelreda in 673, rebuilt in 970. Benedictine Abbot Simon (relative of William I) rebuilt again from 1083 onwards. Existing transepts and nave, c. 1100–40, with fine proportions but severely unornamented. Prior's doorway and other to cloister, c. 1160, richly carved. W front and W tower probably of c. 1150 (some parts altered). Chancel C13, crossing and central tower (octagon) C14. *Monastic buildings:* fragmentary Norman work in undercroft of *Prior's House* (now part of King's School), *storehouse* doorway, c. 1180, bits of the *infirmary*, c. 1180, and its *chapel*

(whose chancel is now a room in the Deanery), undercroft of *Cellarer's House*, doorway of *Walsingham House*, undercroft of the *Almonry* (all these in the precinct). *St Mary*, nearby, has fine Transitional interior, 1198–1215, with zigzag and pointed arches.

Escomb, County Durham. Now among trees in council housing-estate at Escomb, NW of Bishop Auckland, complete small early Anglo-Saxon church of *St John* (20, *20,* 21), c. 680. Impressive masonry outside, with some later windows inserted in 1 wall for daylight within. Inside, high narrow white nave, intriguing chancel arch and square (small but lofty) chancel. Off chancel and nave, 3 probable *porticus* openings (see Chapter 1), 2 of them blocked.

Ewenny Priory, S of Bridgend, Mid Glamorgan. (77, 118, *121*.) Delectable complete Norman priory church, in delightful remote setting, very difficult to find yet quite close to main road. Church founded in c. 1120, priory in 1141. Early Norman nave with arcade. Serene transepts, crossing and ribbed barrel-vaulted chancel, c. 1140–50. Remnants of monastic buildings visible in adjoining house (private).

Ewloe, Clwyd. Village 2 miles SW of Queensferry, *castle* across a field to the N. D-plan keep (55) of c. 1200–10, basement and 1 hall storey only, built by the Welsh. Outer walls and W tower, c. 1250, by Llywelyn ap Gruffydd.

Exeter, Devon. *Cathedral* (100, 123), towers are magnificent blank-arcaded, etc., Norman work of c. 1170, positioned unusually over transepts; cathedral itself all Gothic. *St Mary Arches,* Mary Arches Street, has handsome Norman nave with 2 light arcades of unornamented round piers with double-chamfered arches, but E end Gothic. *St Mary Steps,* West Street, has Norman font. *St Nicholas Priory,* in The Mint, has remains partly open to public, partly in a school. Various Norman walls and undercroft, c. 1100, also carved C10 shaft of Saxon cross. *St Stephen,* High Street, early C19 church with blocked Norman crypt beneath. *Rougemont Castle,* Norman main Gatehouse Tower and other parts survive with walls around C18 Assize Courts, etc.

Eyam, Derbyshire. In churchyard, spiralled shaft and figure-sculptured top of Mercian *cross* (23), c. 800 (upper shaft partly lost).

Eynsford, Kent. Unique *castle* (45), with early Norman flint wall of c. 1090 around low wide earthen motte, which first had small timber tower and dwellings (tufa garderobes survive), then the stone 'Hall-house' of c. 1140 whose undercroft (83) survives.

Farleigh, Surrey. Simple *church* (61) of c. 1100, nave and chancel, little ornament, in pretty village.

Felixkirk, North Yorkshire. *Church* with apsed chancel, arches with zigzag and beakhead, c. 1130–40, nave with Norman arcades, but all over-restored in 1860.

Fingest, Buckinghamshire. *Church* (63)

has tall and massive tower of c. 1060–80 (space within probably providing the original nave) and tiny early Norman nave (originally the chancel?) plus C14 chancel.

Fishlake, South Yorkshire. Largely post-Norman *church* with 1 famous 4-order figure-sculpted (plus animals and foliage) S doorway, c. 1190.

Ford, West Sussex. Charming rustic *church,* much of it late Saxon or earliest Norman, with some later work.

Forde (or Ford) Abbey, Dorset. This major Cromwellian, etc., country house incorporates (with later decoration) the Norman chapter house, c. 1150, of famous Cistercian monastery as its chapel. Some of its arches have zigzag – odd for a Cistercian building.

Forncett St Peter, Norfolk. *Church* (39, *39*), with lovely Anglo-Danish circular tower, c. 1020–60, several round windows, twin bell-openings. Church walls have herringbone masonry of c. 1060. Inside, tall narrow tower arch, but the rest rebuilt.

Forres, Grampian Region. *Sueno's Stone,* carved cross (shaft only) 23 ft high, c. 900?

Foston, North Yorkshire. *Church* has notable S doorway, c. 1150–60, with figure-sculpture medallions, also some furnishings.

Fountains Abbey, North Yorkshire. (103, 104, 105, *106, 107,* 125.) The most famous Cistercian monastic ruin in Britain, and justly so (but see under Byland, Kirkstall and Rievaulx for other dramatic Yorkshire monasteries). Fully described and illustrated in Chapter 5. Founded 1132, ruined abbey church, c. 1135–47, E range cloister (with chapter house), c. 1160, S cloister range (with refectory, etc.), c. 1170–1205, W cloister range (with lay-brothers' buildings), c. 1170–1205, guest-houses, c. 1170–1210; the rest later and more ruined.

Fownhope, Hereford and Worcester. Largely C13 *church* has Norman tower with zigzagged arched space inside, and exquisite tympanum (now inside church) of Virgin and Child, c. 1150, of Shobdon (q.v.) style.

Framlingham, Suffolk. Experimental late Norman *castle* (57, *58*) of type brought from the East by returning Crusaders. No keep, but high curtain wall punctuated by many large wall-towers (traces of original domestic buildings within walls). Built in c. 1190–1210 by Earl of Norfolk (a Bigod), restored to favour (see under Bungay and Orford), on site of earlier Bigod family castle destroyed by Henry II in 1174.

Freiston, Lincolnshire. *Priory church* (Benedictine), nave and crossing arch, c. 1120–80, survive inside later work.

Freswick, Highland Region. Remains of village of Norse settlers' *Long Houses* (80), c. 1000 (one with steam sauna bathroom), like Jarlshof (q.v.).

Fritton, Suffolk. Pretty *church* with Norman round tower, tunnel-vaulted chancel and still thatched. Nave rebuilt later.

Furness Abbey, Cumbria. Spectacular ruins of Cistercian monastery, just NE of Barrow-in-Furness, include church transepts, c. 1180, round-arched cloister ranges and entrance to chapter house (early C13), plus monks' reredorter.

Garton-on-the-Wolds, Humberside. *Church* has high Norman tower (top later) and corbel-tables outside, the interior mostly of c. 1130 with zigzag, but extensively restored in 1850–70 by J. L. Pearson and then G. E. Street (who supervised the now peeling wall-paintings).

Geddington, Northamptonshire. *Church* has remnants of triangular-headed Anglo-Saxon arcading in nave walls. N aisle of c. 1200.

Glastonbury, Somerset. Evocative *abbey* ruins, c. 1185 onwards, of this almost legendary wealthy Benedictine monastery. The best-preserved is *St Mary's Lady Chapel* (75) (1184–6, in luxuriantly carved Transitional style, though eroded) on site of original Anglo-Saxon church there.

Gloucester. *Cathedral* (115, 117, *119*), crypt, ambulatory (with some chapels), and crossing of 1090s survive, and the great nave of c. 1105–20 with soaring drum-piers (vaulting Gothic). Precinct *chapter house* largely Norman. Monks' cemetery not open to public. *St Mary de Crypt,* Southgate Street, has Norman tower, crypt arches and some sculpture. *Fleece Hotel,* Westgate Street, has fine Norman undercroft now called 'Monks Retreat' but probably once part of a rich house. *St Mary Magdalene* (in disuse), in the street called Wotton, is the c. 1150 chancel of chapel for leper hospital.

Gnosall, Staffordshire. *Church* has fine crossing and S transepts, c. 1180.

Goodmanham, Humberside. *Church* (69) thought to be site of pagan temple disrupted by its priest when Northumbrians converted in c. 627 (see Chapter 1). Charming, rather primitive, chancel arch, c. 1120, aisle arcade, c. 1190; the rest post-Norman.

Goodrich, Hereford and Worcester. *Castle* has small keep, c. 1150, 3 storeys, interiors altered, among fine later walls and towers.

Gosforth, Cumbria. Lovely 15 ft tall *Gosforth Cross,* complete with wheel cross-head, c. 980 (in churchyard of partly Norman St Mary's), has interlace carving of Celtic and Viking influences (compare much earlier style at Bewcastle). Various other carved stones of that period are in the church.

Great Paxton, Cambridgeshire. Dull *church* outside, but magnificent interior. Rarest feature is Anglo-Saxon (or Anglo-Danish, here in the Danelaw) true crossing, with 4 equal massive arches of c. 1020. Aisled nave (also a rarity) of same period with unusual piers. Chancel rebuilt Gothic.

Great Shefford, Berkshire. *Church* has round tower (octagonal at top), c. 1100, of type common in East Anglia but unique in this area. Interior has zigzag features apparently altered to pointed arches after 1200. Fine Norman font.

Greensted, Essex. Unique surviving Anglo-Saxon timber *church* (35) (probably the material used for most pre-Conquest churches). Nave built 1013 or earlier, split logs of oak set upright. Tudor chancel and dormer windows. Restored C19.

Guildford, Surrey. *St Mary,* Quarry Street, Anglo-Saxon tower, c. 1060, with traces of splayed windows and lesenes inside. 2 crossing arches, c. 1100, nave with tower arch and 2 chapels, c. 1180, chancel revaulted, c. 1220 (apse vanished).

Gullane, Lothian Region. Among ruins of Norman *church* (St Andrew), now part of graveyard, splendid chancel arch (blocked) with c. 1150 zigzag, and other fragments. Present parish church, 1887, by J. Honeyman, neo-Norman in tribute to past.

Hackness, North Yorkshire. *Church* (27) has chancel arch, c. 1030, S arcade, c. 1130, with rounded simple arches, N arcade Transitional, c. 1200. 2 fragments of fine cross C8 or C9.

Haddon Hall, Derbyshire. Of this famous medieval country mansion, NW tower, parts of chapel and some other wall masonry (e.g. in Peveril's Tower) date from c. 1170, when Vernon family acquired it; the rest later.

Hadleigh, Essex. Norman *church* on noisy main road, with nave, chancel and apse, complete with many original windows.

Hadstock, Essex. Lower parts of c. 1050 *church,* with N doorway, double-splayed windows and transepts (unusual in Anglo-Saxon churches). Upper parts of church Gothic.

Hales, Norfolk. Complete Norman *church,* c. 1150, with round tower, nave and chancel – only a few windows changed. *Heckingham church,* near Hales, has Norman round tower, nave, apsed chancel, c. 1150. Good Norman windows and doorway, and still thatched.

Halesowen, Hereford and Worcester. Splendid largely Gothic *church* with extensive Norman zigzagged and arcaded features still to be seen.

Hampnett, Gloucestershire. *Church* has notable vaulted chancel, c. 1180, decorated by Clayton and Bell, 1871.

Harbledown, Kent. *Chapel* of Hospital of St Nicholas, zigzagged and apsed, beside Victorian almshouses.

Hardham, West Sussex. Rustic early Norman *church* (61, 76), c. 1080s, small nave and chancel, tiny original windows, several replaced by later Gothic ones. Famous but faded wall-paintings perhaps as early as c. 1130 and believed to have been supervised by Cluniac priory of Lewes.

Hastings, East Sussex. By the shore, ruins of *castle* and its collegiate *church* retain masonry of c. 1070 and c. 1170. The rest has fallen into sea.

Haughmond, Shropshire. Ruins of Augustinian Canons' *abbey,* founded c. 1135, include some c. 1160–70 buildings (notably chapter house entrance and refectory) among later work.

Hawkchurch, Devon. *Church* preserves good grotesque-headed Norman corbel-tables, c. 1160, outside, chancel arch and N arcade of nave; the rest C13 and chancel C19.

Healaugh, North Yorkshire. Tower and

small Norman *church* of c. 1140, N aisle, c. 1180.

Heath Chapel, Shropshire. See under Diddlebury.

Heddon-on-the-Wall, Northumberland. Quoins of the *church* are obviously Anglo-Saxon, c. 1020–50, Norman N aisle and fine rib-vaulted chancel.

Helmsley, North Yorkshire. In the town, interesting *castle* of c. 1200, with its keep built as part of curtain wall (rather than within it).

Hemel Hempstead, Hertfordshire. Interesting big Norman *church,* with rib-vaulted chancel, c. 1140 (little carved ornament), transepts and crossing with tower, c. 1160 (spire later), nave enriched by zigzag, etc., c. 1160–80. Many windows now post-Norman.

Hemingford Grey, Cambridgeshire. *Manor House* (82) has as its core the 2-storey manor of c. 1180, with hall on upper floor. Norman door and 3 2-light windows survive. (Private house, write to proprietor re visiting.)

Hereford. *Cathedral* (100, 123, 124), new foundation of c. 1110. S transept partly of c. 1110, chancel with unusual decorated openings and large E arch, c. 1115–30, for apse (apse itself replaced, and E arch and other parts of cathedral over-restored). Crossing, 1130s, and nave, c. 1130–45, when consecrated. Nave, etc., carved ornament has stylistic similarities to Shobdon (q.v.) type, but abstract not figure carving. E end Gothic. *Bishop's Palace,* fragments only of hall, c. 1190, and chapel.

Heversham, Cumbria. *Cross* of perhaps c. 900 in St Peter's churchyard.

Hexham, Northumberland. *Priory church* (20), founded c. 680 by St Wilfrid. 3-chamber crypt of c. 680 survives, of re-used Roman stones and Anglo-Saxon hard cement, with tunnel-vaulted or triangular-headed roof. Also notable bishop's throne, c. 680, Acca's cross, c. 740, and other sculpture fragments. Church itself C13, plus nave of 1907. *Monastery,* priory gate good c. 1160 work, other ruins mostly post-Norman.

Heysham, Lancashire. Ancient oasis on hill overlooking bay, among miles of seaside boarding-houses and Dunroamin. *Parish church* has many C10 or C11 Anglo-Saxon parts (W and N doorways, W window and masonry), good Anglian-Viking hogback tombstone, C10, early Norman chancel arch, and (in

churchyard near outer gate) stump of
Anglian cross showing a building.
Monastery (28), up hill from church, is
older and more magical still. So-called *St
Patrick's Chapel* (*28, 28*) perhaps of early
800s, simple cell with impressive
grooved-arch doorway. Walls of other
monastic buildings and row of rock-cut
graves (rare in Britain).

Hornby, North Yorkshire. *Church*,
tower and its arch of c. 1080, primitive,
chancel and N arcade, c. 1170–80,
octagonal abaci and waterleaf capitals,
but unusually with zigzag.

Horsham St Faith, Norfolk. Norman
entrance to Benedictine monastery
chapter house (the rest vanished)
survives at *Abbey Farm,* N of parish
church.

Horton, Avon. *Horton Court,* beside
village church, has N wing that was
probably the priest's house (or prebend
of Bath or Gloucester?). Ground-floor
hall, with 2 facing zigzagged doorways
with leaf capitals and 2 Norman
windows, c. 1170–80.

Hough-on-the-Hill, Lincolnshire.
Church, lower part of tower, c. 1030,
stair turret outside. Inside, tall thin tower
arch and triangular-headed doorway high
above (for former gallery).

Hovingham, North Yorkshire. *Church,*
tower and W door, c. 1060; the rest
Victorian, though notable figure-
sculpted stone, c. 800, in S aisle.

Huntingdon, Cambridgeshire.
Formerly county town of its own shire.
Cromwell Museum was one end of
Hospital of St John, c. 1180. 2 bays of
original 7 survive, blank arcading, some
zigzag. Restored in 1878.

Icklesham, East Sussex. Norman *church*
started with early tower, c. 1100,
continued with late aisled nave and
chapels, c. 1170–1200, Gothic chancel.

Ickleton, Cambridgeshire. *Church* with
major early Norman crossing and aisled
nave, c. 1100. Chancel Victorian.

Iffley, Oxfordshire. See under Oxford.

Iford, East Sussex. *Church* and tower
largely Norman and Transitional.
Swanborough Manor, ¾ mile NW of
village, has much-altered hall of Norman
house, c. 1200, in N wing. (Private, write
to proprietor for permission to visit.)

Ilam, Staffordshire. In churchyard of
Holy Cross church, the shafts of 2 *crosses,*
C11.

Ilkley, North Yorkshire. 3 Anglian

crosses, c. 850, in churchyard of All
Saints. *Otley church,* 2 miles ESE of
Ilkley, partly Norman, contains work of
c. 850 among 17 pieces of Anglian stone
sculpture.

Inchinnan, Strathclyde Region. In
churchyard, sculpted *stones* and *cross slab*
of C8–10.

Inworth, Essex. Small *church,* Saxon or
very early Norman, with low chancel
arch, splayed windows. Tower, etc.,
Victorian.

Inverurie, Grampian Region. Pictish
symbol *stones,* c. 800?

Iona, Inner Hebrides. Monastic
community founded in 563 by St
Columba, an Irish prince, bringing
Christianity to Scotland. Some early
earthworks and traces of *monk's cell* (13)
on a hillock, near cathedral, are
attributed to Columba's time. Also near
cathedral, 3 *crosses* (22) – St Martin's,
c. 950–1000, St John's (replica of broken
original, which is in museum with other
stones), and St Matthew's (lower shaft
only), a little later. In cathedral precinct,
the tiny *St Oran's Chapel* (77), Scottish-
Norman Romanesque of c. 1180, and
some features of same style in
Benedictine *nunnery church* ruins nearer
village. *Cathedral* itself basically C13,
enlarged 1499 onwards when given
cathedral status.

Irton, Cumbria. Anglo-Saxon *cross,*
c. 900?, in St Paul's churchyard.

Islay, Inner Hebrides. At Kildalton, the
well-preserved carved *Kildalton Cross*
(22), notable work of c. 950–1000.

Isleham, Cambridgeshire. *Priory church*
has excellent austere early Norman nave,
c. 1090, with chancel and apse retaining
small windows and herringbone
masonry. (NB: parish church is post-
Norman.)

Jarlshof, Shetland. Remains of *village* of
Norse settlers' houses (81), c. 800–1000,
on Sumburgh Head, S tip of Shetland.
Small early houses were enlarged to 8
70 ft Long Houses, with walls of earth
core with drystone facings inside and
outside (see also under Birsay and
Freswick).

Jarrow, Tyne and Wear. *St Paul,* c. 684,
in industrial suburb, signposted from
town approaches. Bede the historian
lived and died here in 735. Recent
research (by Dr H. M. Taylor) suggests
the Victorian nave replaces original St
Paul's (18) of c. 684, but present chancel

was St Mary's (18, *19*), of c. 690, a 2nd church aligned E–W as at C7 Canterbury (q.v.), these having been joined in late Anglo-Saxon times and that junction crowned by the early Norman tower – in c. 1075–80, by a Saxon monk who revived the monastery (94) for a few years, but then the brothers were sent to Durham. Evocative *monastery buildings'* remains are probably C10, including good triangular-headed doorway. See also under Sunderland (Monkwearmouth).

Jedburgh, Borders Region. Augustinian *abbey* (124), founded 1138 by David I for Canons from France, now imposing ruin in town centre, choir and crossing, c. 1150, walls survive, lower parts of nave and W front, c. 1190. Nave and monastic ruins C13 onwards.

Jervaulx Abbey, North Yorkshire. (103.) Cistercian abbey, founded here 1156. Very slight remains of church, apparently c. 1180–1200, with 1 imposing wall surviving. Of extensive ruins, cellar entrance is Norman; the rest C13 and later.

Jevington, East Sussex. *Church,* with stubby Saxon tower and tower arch, with notable relief carving of Christ riding.

Keills, Strathclyde Region. Stone *cross,* c. 1000.

Kelso, Borders Region. Dramatic remains towering in town centre are W end (with W transepts) of double-cruciform *abbey church* (124, *166*), c. 1180–1200 (of a reformed Benedictine order founded in c. 1126). Transitional architecture, basically Romanesque still.

Kempley, Gloucestershire. Older of the 2 churches (the other important Arts and Crafts) is *St Mary,* major monument with tunnel-vaulted chancel of c. 1100 (notable frescoes probably of c. 1180), zigzagged chancel arch and S doorway with fine Dymock-style (q.v.) carving.

Kenilworth, Warwickshire. *Castle,* among romantic post-Norman ruins Henry II's big square keep (48), c. 1170 (with angle-turrets), survives. *Church* has ornate doorway, c. 1180, beakhead and battlemented arches.

Kerry, Powys. Can be spelt Ceri. *Churchyard* is circular, sign of a Celtic *clas* monastery. In mostly later *church* (77), arcade of c. 1170 piers and round arches, primitively simple for its date.

Kildalton, Inner Hebrides. See under Islay.

Kilkhampton, Cornwall. *Church* has S doorway of c. 1150, with 4 orders of beakhead, zigzag, etc.

Kilpeck, Hereford and Worcester. Superb *church* (*64, 70, 76, 77, 124*), for its architecture and sculpture – nave, chancel and vaulted apse all of c. 1140–50, intact except a few altered windows. The c. 1150 carving of belfry, W window, corbel-tables, S doorway (especially), and internally of chancel arch, etc., is by the Shobdon (q.v.) master – intricately twining trails and figures and many other motifs delicately executed. *Castle* (52), in field beside church, sparse fragments of polygonal shell-keep on small motte. *Rowlstone church,* 5 miles SW, has spectacular carving on chancel arch and S doorway with tympanum of Shobdon type.

Kirby Cane, Norfolk. *Church,* round tower Anglo-Danish, c. 1020, lesene-strips on lower part. Norman chancel and nave with doorway, c. 1180, but many Gothicised features.

Kirk Hammerton, North Yorkshire. Almost complete Anglo-Saxon *church* of c. 1050. High slim W tower, tower arch, S door, nave (now S aisle of later church), chancel arch and chancel; N aisle added in c. 1200. Megalithic masonry visible outside, incorporated into late Victorian church.

Kirkburn, Humberside. *Church* (65, 67), c. 1140, nave with corbel-table outside and Norman windows. Some post-Norman work and the whole restored by J. L. Pearson, 1856. Wild and primitively sculpted Norman font.

Kirkby Lonsdale, Cumbria. *Church* (69, *70*) has notable N arcade of Durham-type incised round piers, c. 1120. Late Transitional chancel E end with 3 lancets, c. 1200, plus other C12 features among later work.

Kirkdale, North Yorkshire. 2 miles SW of Kirkby Moorside, isolated late Anglo-Saxon *church* by river. Nave, tower arch and chancel arch, c. 1060, arcade, c. 1190, Transitional, chancel and tower C19. Anglian cross, tomb-covers and wall sundial.

Kirkham Priory, North Yorkshire. (102.) On border of Humberside. Augustinian Canons' foundation of c. 1125. Lovely setting, ruins include Norman walls with few features, but 1 magnificent doorway, c. 1190, with bold carving including large lozenge pattern.

Kelso Abbey church ruins (c. 1180–1200), in the Borders of Scotland

Kirkliston, Lothian Region. *Church* has late Norman tower and nave, perhaps c. 1190, free of decoration except scalloped capitals.

Kirkmadrine, Dumfries and Galloway Region. Several inscribed *stones*, one of C5, are in outer wall of church.

Kirkstall Abbey, West Yorkshire. (103.) In NW suburb of Leeds. Founded c. 1152, among the most splendid of Cistercian abbeys (see Chapter 5, also under Byland, Fountains and Rievaulx among other Yorkshire monasteries). Impressive ruins show buildings mostly of c. 1155–75, the church still of simple Cistercian plan (unlike the later Byland),

and retaining 1 side of its crossing tower, with the order's typical mixture of pointed with round arches and corbels, etc. (though scalloped, not waterleaf, capitals). Cloister very ruined, but some waterleaf capitals. Chapter house partly c. 1170, partly C13. Remains of parlatorium C12, altered later. Many other buildings C13–15.

Kirkwall, Mainland, Orkney. The only complete Romanesque *cathedral* (124) in Scotland and very beautiful. Quite small, started by Norse Earl Rognvald in 1137, dedicated to his 'martyred' uncle St Magnus, perhaps employing Norman masons. Red sandstone, chancel,

c. 1137–80, crossing and nave, c. 1180 onwards, completed C15 with vaulting still Romanesque in feeling and simplest Gothic W front.

Knook, Wiltshire. Tiny *church* with Saxon carving by altar, earliest Norman tympanum over doorway; the rest Norman though chancel arch altered by W. Butterfield, 1874.

Lambourn, Berkshire. Handsome Norman *church* has nave, aisles and crossing, c. 1160–80, crossing arches Transitional pointed, nave arcades round arches. Norman W front with ornately carved late Norman doorway, lozenged and animal motifs in arches. Transepts and chancel Gothic.

Lancaster. Big Norman *keep* survives within the prison, but cannot be visited.

Lanercost, Cumbria. NW of Carlisle, *Lanercost Priory* (Augustinian), partly in use, partly ruined church of c. 1170–90 (Transitional features) and C13, plus some monastic remains with post-Dissolution house, C16, added.

Langford, Oxfordshire. *Church,* tower of c. 1050 with tower arch and sculpture of exceptional sophistication for Anglo-Saxon. Nave aisles, c. 1200, Transitional. Notable 'crucifixus' sculpture in porch is Anglo-Saxon of 900s.

Lanherne, at Mawgan in Pydar, near Newquay, Cornwall. By main entrance to Lanherne House (now convent) in Mawgan village, splendid figure-carved *cross* of 900s.

Lastingham, North Yorkshire. Haunting *church* on edge of moors. Monastery founded by St Cedd in 654, destroyed by Vikings C9. Cross-head, c. 850, in crypt. Memorable crypt, apse and 1 bay of chancel built by monks from Whitby, c. 1078–85, after which they went to York. Well restored by J. L. Pearson, c. 1880.

Launceston, Cornwall. Round *shell-keep* (45) of stone, c. 1200, with later high round tower within its walls, on earlier partly artificial motte in town centre (S gatehouse may be c. 1200 too). *St Thomas* nearby has strange Norman font and tympanum.

Ledsham, North Yorkshire. E of Leeds. Major Anglo-Saxon *church,* 2-storey W porch, nave, 1 *porticus* now main entrance, traces of N *porticus,* dates ranging from before 800 to c. 1050 (e.g. tower doorway). Tower over W porch Norman, the top c. 1400.

Leek, Staffordshire. 2 Mercian *crosses* of c. 1050 stand in churchyard of St Edward the Confessor church, plus 2 fragments in chancel and porch.

Legerwood, Borders Region. *Church* has richly ornate arch, c. 1150.

Leicester. *Castle,* earthen motte of c. 1070. Within *Court House* (c. 1700) in Castle Yard, part of Norman Great Hall, c. 1160 – parts of walls, windows, timber roof and wooden capital of vanished arcade. *St Mary in Castro,* Castle Yard, started in 1107, disappointing spatially but fine detail. Ornate doorways, c. 1160, as is noted triple sedilia. *All Saints,* Highcross Street, lower tower and zigzagged doorways, c. 1150. *St Nicholas,* near excavated Roman walls, Anglo-Saxon nave, c. 700–50, parts of chancel and 2 windows. Imposing tower, c. 1100 and (above) c. 1130. Doorways, arcaded nave, 1 window and sedilia, c. 1130–60, with Victorian restoration.

Lenton, Nottinghamshire. In NW suburbs of Nottingham. Victorian *church,* on site of Cluniac monastery, contains major sculpted Norman font.

Leominster, Hereford and Worcester. *Priory church* (117), 1121–c. 50, fine stern arcaded nave, but chancel vanished and 2nd nave, aisle and tower post-Norman. Ornate figure sculpture in W portal (123), c. 1160.

Leuchars, Fife Region. The best-known and, with Dalmeny (q.v.), the best Romanesque *church* (77, 78) in Scotland. Nave, chancel and apse, linked to de Quinci family of nearby castle (motte only now). Date of church is a puzzle – a church was here by 1187, but other documents suggest more building in 1190s. Interior has impressive dark spaces, tall stern chancel and apse arches, though enriched by zigzag, etc. Exterior of apse and chancel, in contrast, festive with intersecting or enriched blank arcades in 2 tiers all round, and carved corbel-table heads. But style looks more of 1160s than 1190s.

Lewannick, Cornwall. 2 *stones* (1 in church, 1 in churchyard) inscribed partly in Latin, partly in Celtic Ogham script, probably of 600s.

Lewes, East Sussex. *Castle,* remains of Norman shell-keep and gatehouse, c. 1100. *St Pancras Priory,* off Cockshut Road, scant remains of great Cluniac Benedictine monastery (94) founded by William I's great baron William de

Warenne in 1077, introducing the reformed art-loving Order to England (see Chapter 5 and under Reading). Of the long priory church (which had radiating apsed chapels at E, like Cluny itself) only part of SW tower remains. Railway now across cloister site, but a corner of refectory (herringbone wall and splayed windows, indicating c. 1080), vault below vanished round lavatorium (wash-room), traces of chapel and dormitory undercroft of 1100s can be seen. (Fine carved capitals, c. 1140, from priory are in Lewes Museum and British Museum, London.) *St John*, St John's Hill, below castle, Saxon doorway set in Victorian church. *St Michael*, High Street, round tower, probably Norman. *St Anne*, at top of High Street, Norman tower, nave and 1 transept, much altered. Splendid S arcade, c. 1190, Transitional, stiff-leaf (typically Gothic) capitals, 1 arch round, others pointed. Norman font.

Lincoln. See Chapter 4 for suggested walk. *High Street*, 3 churches along its 1-mile length, below cathedral hill, with late Anglo-Saxon towers – *St Benedict, St Peter-at-Gowts* (which has other Anglian and Norman features too) and *St Mary-le-Wigford* (which also has Anglian inscribed stone). *Cathedral* (100, 123, *123*) started by Bishop Remigius in c. 1075, dedicated in 1092. All rebuilt Gothic except 3 tall arches of Remigius's W front (74), their lower sculpted round portals and sculpture bands of 1140s, lower parts of W towers, 1140s. In the precinct, *Deloraine Court* in James Street has Norman undercroft. Ruined *Bishop's Palace*, S of cathedral, has remains of Great Hall, c. 1200. *Castle* (45) has, among extensive later buildings, well-preserved shell-keep, c. 1180, on tree-covered motte, parts of Observatory Tower, much of curtain walls and 2 gateways are Norman. Norman houses: *Norman House* (88, *89*), Steep Hill (street from cathedral precinct gateway down to High Street), of c. 1170–80, with re-made 2-light window but other original features (formerly wrongly called Aaron's House). Down the hill, in The Strait, the famous *Jew's House* (88, *90*), c. 1170–80, with original doorway, windows and chimney-breast (details somewhat damaged by time, ground-floor storerooms now shops). Downhill again and at far end of High Street, *St*

Mary's Guild (90, *91*) on left, c. 1180–90, imposing stone frontage, windows and doors and big courtyard entrance arch (formerly wrongly called John of Gaunt's Stables).

Lindisfarne (Holy Island), Northumberland. Celtic *monastery* (13, 27) founded from Iona (q.v.) by St Aidan in 635, later the house of the much-loved St Cuthbert (who was outwitted by Rome's St Wilfrid at Synod of Whitby in 664, but for whose miraculous uncorrupt remains Durham cathedral was built). Reached by causeway at low tide. Ruins now are of the great Norman Benedictine priory (115) that replaced earlier buildings in c. 1110–40. Foundations only of apsed chancel, but moving remains of nave, c. 1120–40, with fine but eroded drum-piers of Durham type, incised in large patterns. Monastic remains mostly C13 onwards.

Linley, Shropshire. *Church*, reached up a drive from Linley Hall, has Norman tower, corbel-table, tower space, nave and chancel, plus font and wild N tympanum.

Little Missenden, Buckinghamshire. *Church*, Anglo-Saxon traces in chancel arch and nave. Notable wall-paintings of c. 1190 forming partial dado along N and S sides of nave (plus a St Christopher and 5 scenes involving St Catherine and the passion of Christ, all C13).

Little Saxham, Suffolk. *Church*, fine round tower of c. 1130, with intricate arcading at bell stage. Tall tower arch inside, but church itself rebuilt.

Littleborough, Nottinghamshire. *Church*, c. 1070–80, minute, unaisled nave, much herringbone work in walls, simple chancel arch.

Llanbadarn Fawr, Powys. *Church* is largely Victorian neo-Norman, but preserves 2-order S doorway, c. 1150, sculpted capitals, zigzagged and hood-moulded arch, relief-sculpted tympanum of 2 lions looking hungrily at Tree of Life – perhaps by pupil of Shobdon (q.v.) school.

Llanddewi Brefi, Dyfed. Large *church*, crossing tower and chancel late Norman, nave Victorian, on site of famous sermon by St David (or Dewi) in late 500s. Several Ogham script stones inside and on outer walls.

Llaneilian, Anglesey. *Church* has Norman tower, pyramid-topped like

Penmon (q.v.), pretty interior later.

Llanelltud, Gwynedd. Small *church* in ancient circular *clas* churchyard, scant Norman traces in successful architectural *mélange*.

Llangadwaladr, Anglesey. Cadwaladr, a canonised king, built *church* here in c. 630 and most interesting part is the spectacular inscribed gravestone of his grandfather, Cadfan, set in wall of nave (which has Norman stonework, but all architectural features altered). (Key from a nearby house.)

Llanrhwydrys, Anglesey. Tiny *church* (78) in remote corner of island, across field from a farmhouse W of Cemlyn Bay along seashore lanes. Nave of C13 masonry, most windows altered, but with astonishing cruck-frame structure inside and remains of circular *clas* churchyard around.

Llantony, Gwent. 10 miles N of Abergavenny. Famous *monastic ruin* for its setting. Founded 1103 for Augustinian Canons. Walls of crossing and nave of priory church, c. 1175–1230, stand, with some monastic buildings' remnants.

Llantwit Major, South Glamorgan. *St Illtud's Church*, on site where he founded a collegiate institution in c. 500. Huge Norman church (or rather, 2 linked churches) restored from Norman ruins by G. E. Halliday, c. 1890. Carved shaft of Illtud's cross and other important Celtic carved stones are in W part.

LONDON

Central London
Westminster Abbey, only piers and vaulting of Chapel of the Pyx and cloister rooms now housing abbey's museum, plus odd sections of wall elsewhere, survive of the early Norman work of c. 1090. *Tower of London* (46, 47, 48, 52), massive keep (White Tower), a 4-storey 'hall keep', with main hall and many apartments (3 per floor) and galleries, c. 1078–97. Many windows altered in c. 1700. Curved projection on E contains complex little *Chapel of St John* (62, 63), c. 1090. Norman masonry in ruined tower beside keep and elsewhere, but curtain walls started after 1200. *Westminster Hall* (46), only parts of massive stone E and W walls survive of William Rufus's Hall of 1095 (same size as today). *St Mary-le-Bow*, Cheapside,

City, has crypt of c. 1100 or before. *St Bartholomew-the-Great* (117), off Smithfield Market, City, is the chancel (with lovely apsed arcade) plus crossing and transepts (nave vanished) of major Augustinian priory church, founded by Norman magnate Rahere in 1123 and built in c. 1125–35. 1 of the 3 radiating ambulatory chapels (behind apse) survives. Little ornamental carving, but sophisticated and graceful arcade detailing, showing French Romanesque influence. Upper levels Gothic. Restored from ruin by Sir Aston Webb in 1890s. *Temple Church* (77), Temple, off Fleet Street, one of the round-naved churches modelled on Holy Sepulchre Church, Jerusalem, under influence of the Knights Templar following 1st Crusade (for others see under Cambridge, Northampton and Orphir). Eroded portico under porch and circular nave (restored after 1940s bombing), c. 1160–80, with Transitional pointed arches.

Outer London
East Ham: *St Mary Magdalene*, High Street South, basically Norman church inside later exterior. Nave, windows, doorways, chancel and apse, c. 1140, with alterations.

Harlington (formerly in Middlesex): *church* retains Norman nave and splendid doorway, c. 1160.

Laleham (formerly in Middlesex): *church's* arcaded nave, c. 1120, survives; the rest rebuilt later.

St Pancras: old *parish church*, Pancras Road (N of railway station), has Norman fragments in doorway of Victorian neo-Norman church.

Stepney: *St Dunstan*, parish church (C15), contains in S aisle Anglo-Saxon relief carving of Crucifixion with draped figures, perhaps c. 1020.

Long Marton, Cumbria. Attractive *church* (65) with earliest Norman parts (see tower interior, doorways and carving) that show traces of Anglo-Saxon craftsmen at work after Conquest. Upper tower and chancel later Norman. 2 primitively dotty tympana.

Long Sutton, Lincolnshire. *Church* has lengthy Norman nave and chancel arch, c. 1180.

Longtown, Hereford and Worcester. *Castle* (56), splendid circular keep of c. 1200 with large rounded buttresses, windows altered in c. 1400.

Lowther, Cumbria. *Church,* nave arcades of c. 1170 and 1200, Anglo-Norse hogback tombstones in porch; the rest Gothic.

Ludlow, Shropshire. *Castle (50)* has big gatehouse-keep, c. 1110 (entry blocked off later), and inner bailey walls possibly of same date, also chapel (51, 77) of c. 1140 with circular nave (walls stand roofless, while its former chancel and polygonal apse can only be traced by outlines on the grass) among extensive later buildings.

Lullington, Somerset. *Church,* splendid c. 1150 sculpture on tower-space arches inside, on S door and especially N doorway – ornate shafts, animal capitals, tympanum with Tree of Life and zodiac creatures, arches with projecting zigzag and beakhead, hood-mould with seated Christ above. Font is sculpted too.

Lydd, Kent. Grand Gothic *church* of 1300s with several blocked probably Anglo-Saxon arches, clerestory window and remnants of *porticus* in NW corner. Date of this small church either 600s or perhaps Romano-British of 400s.

Lydford, Devon. *Castle* in village has good earthworks, bailey and low motte, and boring little stone keep of 1195.

Lyme Regis, Dorset. Nave and crossing tower of Norman *church* are now W porch and W tower of later Gothic church.

Lyminge, Kent. Gothic *church* (17) with traces (beside porch outside) of St Aethelburga's (daughter of Aethelbert and Bertha, see Chapter 1) mixed monastery of 633, and extensive remains of church rebuilt in c. 960 in walls and windows.

Lyminster, West Sussex. Impressive nave and chancel of Anglo-Saxon *nunnery church* – plain, tall and narrow. Norman additions and the whole encased in gorgeous roof of 1200s.

Mallerstang, Cumbria. *Pendragon Castle,* under 1 mile N of village, is one of the first pele-towers, c. 1200 (much ruined, despite rebuilding in 1660), that is, defended single-tower dwellings later widespread on both sides of the border.

Malmesbury, Wiltshire. *Abbey church,* major Norman monument, built over that made famous by St Aldhelm (see under Bradford-on-Avon) in early 700s. Nave of Benedictine monks' abbey church survives as parish church, c. 1160 onwards, with arcades with pointed arches, but Romanesque billet and zigzag ornament. S portico of great splendour, c. 1160–70, sculpted tympanum and 5 orders with running interlace, medallions and figure sculpture (much smashed) of fine workmanship, as on W doorway.

Malton (Old), North Yorkshire. *Priory* (108) (Gilbertine, see Chapter 5), founded c. 1150. Ruined nave, part of W front, and refectory undercroft (now under C18 Abbey House) all of c. 1180–1200, Transitional.

Manningford Bruce, Wiltshire. Almost complete early Norman *church* of c. 1080–90, though several windows enlarged. Unaisled nave, chancel arch, chancel and apse within, herringbone masonry visible outside. Well restored by J. L. Pearson, 1882.

Manorbier, Dyfed. *Castle* (45), c. 1140, stone tower outside (later) gatehouse and Hall block survive (Hall itself was on 1st floor, the usual Norman domestic plan, and ran up 2 storeys) in fine ruins, with later curtain wall and other buildings. *Church,* on far side of valley from castle, impressive Norman nave, with later arcades and chancel.

Margam, West Glamorgan. Of the Cistercian *abbey,* founded 1147, grand nave (architecturally simple, according to Cistercian rule) and more ornate late Norman. W front survives, with extraordinary C19 additions.

Margate, Kent. *St John the Baptist* has very long Norman nave and chancel.

Marton (West), North Yorkshire. Victorianised Norman church of *St Peter* contains cross of c. 1050 with Viking-style interlace and human figures.

Masham, North Yorkshire. Finely sculpted Anglo-Saxon *cross's shaft* outside basically Norman (lower tower and tower arch) church, much Victorianised.

Mathon, Hereford and Worcester. *Church* has early Norman nave with herringbone masonry, chancel of c. 1160 is square-ended (replacing apse).

Meifod, Powys. Large churchyard was site of Celtic *clas* monastery, but earliest traces now are of arches and a pier, c. 1150, blocked into S wall of nave in largely C13–15 *church.* The really remarkable feature is sculpted slab cross (22) (figure of Christ on cross), probably c. 900, of primitive power, in S aisle.

Meigle, Tayside Region. Collection of Pictish symbol *stones* and *carvings* of

C7–9, in Museum.

Melbourne, Derbyshire. Major Norman *church*, though incomplete towers make exterior unimpressive. But interior has splendid 6-bay aisled nave (drum-piers, stilted arches, much zigzag), crossing with primitive sculpted capitals, tower lantern and chancel (apse rebuilt square-ended C14), all c. 1135–50.

Middleham, North Yorkshire. On road from Richmond to Skipton. Vast *keep* of c.1170 with curtain walls, plus later work.

Milborne Port, Somerset. Magnificent and mysterious *church* (65, *65*). Anglo-Saxon features include W end lesenes, triangular arches, tall narrow doorway and chancel – but perhaps built just post-1066 for Norman masters. Superb Norman crossing and doorway with fat roll-mouldings, c. 1100, plus unusual stairway turret outside. Nave Gothic. *House* in village main street has extraordinary ornate doorway (88, *88*), probably of c. 1200.

Mildenhall, Wiltshire. Little *church* blending many periods beautifully. Tower windows Saxon, tower arch (inside) early Norman, chancel masonry and nave, round-topped arcade, c. 1160, chancel arch Transitional pointed, c. 1190, chancel the same, but most windows Gothic and notably complete Georgian Gothic furnishings.

Minster-in-Sheppey, Kent. Much remains of St (Queen) Sexburga's *nunnery church* of c. 670 in lower walls of present church of 1300s. Parish church beside it, St Mary, is of c. 1230. Monastery excavated, but invisible now.

Minster-in-Thanet, Kent. *St Mary's abbey church,* 1150–1230, and some notable Norman secular buildings among those of modern Minster Abbey nunnery.

Moccas, Hereford and Worcester. Almost complete, severe but grand early Norman *church* (61), c. 1110–20, but with some minimal zigzag appearing. Remote location 12 miles W of Hereford up River Wye.

Monks Horton, Kent. W portal and dormitory range of c. 1180 survive of *Horton Priory,* Cluniac.

Monkwearmouth, Tyne and Wear. See under Sunderland.

Morcott, Leicestershire. *Church,* tower and interior largely Norman of c. 1110, though with many altered features and S

aisle of c. 1200.

Morland, Cumbria. Lower part of *church tower,* c. 1060, is only surviving Anglo-Saxon building in Cumbria (in strange contrast to the many stone crosses). Late Norman nave.

Morwenstow, Cornwall. *Church* has nave arcade, c. 1150, beakhead and zigzag, and other carving on S doorway. Rough font.

Much Wenlock, Shropshire. Ruins of Cluniac *priory* (94) include ornate wall of chapter house and impressive figure sculpture in lavatorium, c. 1180. *Holy Trinity,* priory's separate parish church nearby, has grand Norman nave and chancel, plus tower of c. 1200, and remarkable W wall, outside and in, decorated with zigzag and arcading, c. 1170.

Mylor, near Falmouth, Cornwall. Tall abstract-ornamented *cross* in churchyard of 800s?

Netheravon, Wiltshire. *Church* Gothic, but W tower Anglo-Saxon, c. 1060, with blocked *porticus* on both sides, herringbone masonry, some Norman detail on tower arch inside. Perhaps started before, finished after, the Conquest – or earlier central tower re-used in Norman W end.

New Romney, Kent. *Church* has fine tower, enriched W front and aisled nave of c. 1160. Chancel rebuilt.

Newark, Nottinghamshire. *Castle,* beside river, built in c. 1170–80 by Bishop of Lincoln. Norman ruins include good N gatehouse, with chapel, SW tower and crypt below W range; the rest mostly C14. *St Mary Magdalene,* notable vaulted crypt, c. 1180, under sanctuary.

Newbald, Humberside. Noble Norman *church* (*74,* 76), though many altered windows make E exterior look later. But corbel-table, buttressed walls and doorways (especially S door with Christ in part-*vesica* sculpture above it) are excellent c. 1140 work. Inside, fine Norman crossing, with zigzagged arches, and nave.

Newcastle-upon-Tyne, Tyne and Wear. *Castle* (48), Henry II's royal keep of 1172–7, the North's 'new castle', is still there with its fine chapel. Rest of castle demolished by railway company for their station and lines. *St Nicholas,* chancel arch (2 orders of zigzag) and arcaded nave, c. 1120–30, lower part of tower Norman too, re-using Roman masonry.

Newminster, Northumberland. 1 mile W of Morpeth, fragmentary remains of Cistercian *abbey*, founded 1137, buildings of c. 1180 (parts of church and chapter house).

Newport, Gwent. *St Woolos Cathedral,* on town hilltop, was Benedictine abbey. W doorway (inside, between W Lady Chapel and nave) primitive work of c. 1150, good nave, later 1100s. Later work and restorations disastrous.

Newton, Grampian Region. *The Newton Stone,* Pictish of c. 800?

Nith Bridge, Dumfries and Galloway Region. Shaft of stone *high cross,* C10.

Norham, Northumberland. *Church,* chancel and splendid nave arcade, still with zigzag but waterleaf capitals and octagonal abaci so c. 1180; the rest neo-Norman, 1846. *Castle* (48), Bishop of Durham's superb 3-storey hall-keep is well-preserved c. 1160, 2 upper storeys added C15.

North Elmham, Norfolk. Ruins of Anglo-Danish cathedral of c. 1000 lie N of Gothic parish church. *Cathedral,* quite small, was seat of bishops of Norfolk, c. 800–1075 (see under Norwich). High narrow aisleless nave of big stone blocks. W tower with its projecting round stair turret. Single transept lies right across E end of nave (forming T plan), with apsed E side. Towers stood at corners on nave and transept angles. No chancel as such. Manor-house of 1380s (now also ruined) was built over E part of nave and 1 side of transept, confusing the remains.

North Leigh, Oxfordshire. Anglo-Saxon tower, originally in centre of *church* of c. 1050 (various remnants still visible), whose chancel was converted into present nave, c. 1190.

North Marden, West Sussex. Tiny remote *church* of c. 1090 near Uppark House. Apsed nave only, rare design. 1 original little window, others later Norman and zigzagged doorway of c. 1140.

Northampton. *Holy Sepulchre* (77), Sheep Street, one of the rare circular-plan naves built early 1100s based on Holy Sepulchre Church in Jerusalem after 1st Crusade (see also under Cambridge, London and Orphir). Rectangular chancel, partly c. 1180. Nave pointed arches substituted in c. 1300. *St Peter,* Marefair Street, c. 1150–60, major Norman church. Sumptuously decorated arches and capitals, with alternating drum and multiple piers, no division between nave and chancel, clerestory with blank arcading. *St Giles,* St Giles' Street, bottom of tower and arches of the crossing are Norman.

Norton, Cleveland (Teesside). In northern suburb of Stockton-on-Tees, *church* has late Anglo-Saxon tower and transepts, c. 990.

Norton Priory, Cheshire. Augustinian ruins include richly arched gateway and undercroft of c. 1180.

Norwich. *Cathedral* (95, *112, 113,* 114), with Durham, the highest achievement of the Norman cathedral builders. Started in 1096 after bishop's seat moved here from North Elmham (q.v.) via Thetford. Apsed chancel, 1096–c. 1110 (roof levels Gothic C14 and C15). Crossing with lofty interior lantern and tower, c. 1105–20 (spire above C13, rebuilt C15), transepts same dates. Nave started in 1115–20 (with 1 pair of massive spiral-carved Durham-type drum-piers), completed by 1145. W front Norman with many later alterations (big W window C15). *Monastic buildings,* in cathedral precinct: *cloister* rebuilt C13, but around it are parts of Norman *refectory* (95), *parlatorium* (95) (now Song School), *infirmary* (95) and tunnel-vaulted *Dark Entry passage* (95). *St Aethelreda,* King Street, Norman round tower, aisleless nave with zigzag band along walls, N doorway. *St Mary,* St Mary Plain, off Oak Street, Anglo-Danish round tower, c. 1020, with triangular-headed bell-openings. *Castle* (48), large rectangular hall-keep, c. 1160, with complex blank-arcaded walls, on earthen motte of c. 1070. Restored in 1833 by Salvin, no original interiors survive (now museum). *Bishop's Palace,* Norman wall and 2 round-headed windows survive in Victorian building. *'Music House'* (87), No. 167 King Street, interior of c. 1200 with rib-vaulted undercroft (the hall above rebuilt). *Lazar House,* 219 Sprowston Road, suburban Norwich. Norman range of hospital of c. 1180 survives, with small windows and 2 simple doorways (now branch public library).

Nunburnholme, Humberside. Shaft of famous figure-carved *Nunburnholme Cross,* c. 1000, in church, which has good Norman zigzagged chancel arch.

Oakham, Leicestershire. *Castle,* famous

Hall (83) is sole surviving building, c. 1180–1200, a splendid space with stone arcaded nave and aisles, waterleaf capitals, round-headed main doorway and steep-pitched timber roof.

Odiham Castle, Hampshire. (52.) W of North Warnborough, near canal. Octagonal late Norman keep (like Chilham, q.v.), 3 storeys, ashlar facing destroyed exposing flint core.

Ogmore, Mid Glamorgan. *Castle* with large rectangular keep, c. 1140–50, by Norman family called de Londres, plus later works.

Old Bewick, Northumberland. *Church* has small but grand interior, c. 1120, with some later alterations.

Old Sarum, Wiltshire. On hilltop to N of Salisbury. Ghost city. Outline of vanished Norman cathedral (c. 1090 and c. 1130) marked on grass amidst earthworks and crumbled castle walls (c. 1130) of Sarum before it moved to Salisbury in 1198–1220.

Ongar, Essex. Chipping Ongar: almost complete small Norman *church*, nave and chancel with some re-used Roman brick (aisle Victorian, roof restored C18). High Ongar: *church* with Norman nave and fantastic doorway, c. 1190.

Orford, Suffolk. *Castle* (51, 52, *52, 53*), by Henry II's 'ingeniator' Alnoth, 1165–7, as base for suppressing rebellious Bigod family at Framlingham (q.v.) and Bungay (q.v.). Finely preserved example of experimental polygonal keep to prevent corner undermining, with circular interiors plus smaller chambers, chapel, etc., in forebuilding and in thickness of walls. Extensive bailey earthworks, but walls vanished. *Church* (70), beside present parish church, eroded roofless arcades with slender incised drum-piers of Durham type, c. 1170.

Ormside, Cumbria. *Church* has S doorway and tower arch, c. 1090, nave arcade, c. 1150, W tower, c. 1190.

Orphir, Mainland, Orkney. Scraps of wall, but plan visible, of rare tiny circular-naved *church* (77), with surviving barrel-vaulted chancel, c. 1130.

Ousden, Suffolk. *Church* with Norman central tower space, nave and doorways (one altered).

Oxford. *St Michael*, Cornmarket, Anglo-Saxon tower, c. 1020, long-and-short work quoins, 2 levels of twin bell-openings. *St Peter-in-the-East*, Queen's Lane, crypt, c. 1130, with some carving, rib-vaulted and zigzagged chancel and nave, c. 1160 (now library of St Edmund Hall, college beside the church). *Castle*, New Road, part of earthen motte, c. 1071, can be visited. Other Norman work (chapel crypt, c. 1080, and 1 wall-tower, c. 1100) lies within modern prison not open to the public. Other churches: *St Aldate, St Cross, St Ebbe, St Andrew* in Headington and *St James* in Cowley have individual good Norman features with carving of c. 1160. *Cathedral* (124, 125, *125*), in Tom Quad, Christ Church, its zigzagged entrance to chapter house sole survivor of building of c. 1130. Cathedral itself built as abbey church, c. 1180–1210, lower parts of aisled nave, crossing (tower above) and square-ended choir. Higher levels post-Norman. *Iffley church* (76, *76*), in old village, now suburb, SE along Iffley Road from Magdalen Bridge. One of the most complete and elaborately carved Norman churches in Britain. Nave, central tower space and chancel all of c. 1170, with zigzagged arches, beakhead and figure sculpture on doorways. Carefully restored in 1856 by J. C. Buckler, who added round W window. *Rectory* nearby has some C12 features inside (private).

Ozleworth, Gloucestershire. *Church*, mostly post-Norman, has rare octagonal central tower, c. 1130–40.

Patrixbourne, Kent. Small *church*, its plain interior (restored by G. G. Scott, 1857) contrasting with gorgeous carving of c. 1180 all around exterior.

Pauntley, Gloucestershire. *Church* has Norman zigzagged chancel arch and chancel. Ornate carved S doorway in style of Dymock (q.v.).

Pawlett, Somerset. *Church* later, but fine S doorway of c. 1150 with carved lozenge, zigzag and beakhead patterns.

Pembroke, Dyfed. Grandest Norman *castle* (56, *56*) in Wales. Large circular keep, c. 1200, vaulted inside. Much of curtain wall and several of its rectangular towers also Norman of c. 1200, but rounded wall-towers and other buildings later.

Penmon, Anglesey. *Priory church* (77, 122, *174*) is finest Norman building in N Wales, set in lyrical surroundings overlooking sea. Cruciform plan with pyramidal-topped central tower. Interior is grave early Norman, c. 1120 (chancel restored), but N transept has ornate intersected arcading, etc., of c. 1170, with Celtic font (originally cross-base?) and carved cross of C10.

Pennant Melangell, near Llangynog, Powys. Up remote valley from main road at Llangynog (key to church and shrine from a house in Llangynog – enquire in shops). In an outhouse at E end of tiny church (post-Norman, but some carvings, etc., of the saint) is reconstructed elegant *shrine* (78, *79*) of c. 1160 over tomb of the C8 Irish princess, St Melangell, who fled here, defied and was protected by a local Welsh prince, started nunnery and became patron saint of hares.

Penrith, Cumbria. Churchyard of *St Andrew* has 2 crosses and Anglo-Norse hogback tombs, all of c. 1000.

Pentlow, Essex. Norman *church* with round tower, nave and apsed chancel (many windows altered).

Pershore, Hereford and Worcester. *Abbey church* still has Norman crossing, S transept, c. 1100, lower levels of nave, c. 1130, and font.

Peterborough, Cambridgeshire. *Cathedral* (27, 122, *122*), monastery founded by King Penda of Mercia in c. 650 and destroyed by Danes, refounded as Benedictine abbey and present church started in c. 1118 (became cathedral in 1541). Choir with apse and aisles, c. 1118–50. Crossing and aisled nave, c. 1160–90 (Gothic W front early C13). So virtually complete Norman interior, alternating round and polygonal piers, arches enriched with zigzag, rising to gallery and clerestory with flat roof. At E beyond apse, the Hedda Stone, a major sculpted sarcophagus of c. 800. *Monastic buildings*: outer *gatehouse*, c. 1190 (but upper parts rebuilt C14) and 2 vaulted rooms nearby in *King's Lodging. Tout Hill* in precinct is earthen motte of c. 1100. *Deanery* (Victorian) has 1 large room with fireplace, c. 1200. *Cellars*, blocked doorways of c. 1150 still visible. At Fletton, village now a suburb of Peterborough, fine Anglo-Saxon (Mercian) carvings (as at Breedon, q.v.) in *St Margaret* (largely Norman, c. 1160). Carvings thought to be fragments of frieze, perhaps from the vanished Mercian Peterborough abbey church, so c. 700–800.

Peterchurch, Hereford and Worcester.

Penmon Priory church (c. 1120–70), Anglesey, North Wales. The north transept with a stone cross of c. 1000 and decorative carving of c. 1170

Major Norman *church* of c. 1120–30, unique in having 4 spaces, progressively smaller from nave to apse. Zigzag only on 2nd of the 3 arches and S door, little other ornament, but spatially superb. *Snodhill Castle,* 1 mile NW towards Dorstone, has ruined polygonal keep of c. 1190, plus later stone towers, on motte with huge earthwork enclosure around.

Peterhead, Grampian Region. *Church* has remains of nave and chancel, c. 1150.

Petersfield, Hampshire. Crossing tower of *church,* c. 1120, handsome arcades and aisles added in c. 1180–90, some waterleaf in capitals. Restored by Sir A. Blomfield, 1875.

Pevensey, East Sussex. *Castle,* big square Norman keep (with unusual diagonal buttresses), c. 1100, in vast 'Saxon Shore' fortress, c. 300, with extensive Roman walls. *Westham church,* nearby, has Norman cruciform plan with apsed chancel and transepts originally apsed too, but much altered.

Peveril, Derbyshire. *Castle,* started by William Peverel, one of Conqueror's great magnates in c, 1080. N curtain wall (herringbone masonry) of that period, as is tower (perhaps chapel) in SE corner. Square keep and NE gatehouse built from 1176 onwards by Henry II after confiscation from Peverels.

Pickering, North Yorkshire. *Castle* includes ruins of tower and small living hall, c. 1180, within inner bailey, shell-keep C13. *Church* has nave arcades, c. 1140 (unmoulded) and c. 1180 (water-leaf capitals). Some pre-Norman sculpture fragments.

Pittington, County Durham. NE of Durham, in hamlet called Hallgarth, is *Pittington church* (69), famous for its spectacular arcade of Durham-type incised and sculpted piers (projecting spirals down 2 of them) and arches with 3-dimensional zigzag. Generally dated c. 1115–20 (see 1st appearance of zigzag at Durham cathedral), but zigzag here and octagonal abaci above the capitals probably indicate date later in the century, c. 1180.

Polesworth, Warwickshire. *Priory church* of Benedictine nuns (St Editha), whose long nave of c. 1130 survives inside later exterior. Fragments of nuns' monastic quarters include Norman doorway to cloister.

Polstead, Suffolk. Fascinating *church* for its brick arches of Norman date (bricks

were not made in England between withdrawal of Romans and about C13, when still very rare). Norman doorway, arcaded nave and chancel arch, c. 1180–1200. Nave arches of bricks, varying in size but about $11 \times 6 \times 1\frac{3}{4}$ in. each, quite different from re-used Roman bricks found elsewhere and seemingly contemporary with rest of building. Possibly imported or else the earliest English manufactured bricks anywhere.

Portchester, Hampshire. *Castle (47,* 48, 118), big and well-preserved keep built in c. 1120 by Henry I (heightened in c. 1160) in one corner of immense C4 Roman fortress to guard 'Saxon Shore'. *Priory church* (118), also within area enclosed by Roman brick walls, founded for Augustinian Canons, c. 1130. Spacious cruciform church with fine crossing arches (billet-pattern carving) survives almost intact (1 transept destroyed).

Portslade, East Sussex. W of Brighton and Hove, beside village church (Norman nave), ruined remains of *manor-house* (82) of late 1100s – 2 walls and round-arched window – in nightmare modern housing development.

Portsmouth, Hampshire. *Cathedral* (originally large parish church) has Transitional-style chancel, c. 1190, of great interest, showing Norman moving into early Gothic.

Prestbury, Cheshire. In churchyard, beyond large parish church, charming small Norman *church* of c. 1160, interior messed about but W front has ornate though eroded sculpture, zigzag and pellet, human beakhead, etc.

Prudhoe, Northumberland. *Castle,* oasis among the coalmines, and high over River Tyne. Gatehouse, c. 1150, and small keep with forebuilding that may be as early as 1100–20.

Pyrford, Surrey. Early Norman village *church* (61), c. 1100, simplest detail inside. Nave, chancel arch and chancel. E window Gothic. Well restored by T. G. Jackson, 1869.

Ramsbury, Wiltshire. In *church,* group of C9 excavated shafts of Saxon crosses, gravestones – one with Viking dragon – and some Norman sculpture.

Ramsey, Cambridgeshire. Abbey, founded c. 970, then on an island for defence. Of abbey church only *Lady Chapel,* c. 1250, remains, but the *Hospitium* (for guests) of c. 1190 is now the impressive parish church, with aisled nave and chancel. Arcades with carved capitals, many windows enlarged later.

Reading, Berkshire. *Reading Abbey,* by Market Place, in almost unrecognisable ruins, remains of great Cluniac monastery (see also under Lewes) founded in c. 1130 by Henry I. Fragments of S transept, tunnel-vaulted slype, chapter house, dormitory, refectory and mill (with arches including a little zigzag). Finely sculpted capitals from abbey can be seen in Reading Museum and Victoria & Albert Museum, London.

Reculver, Kent. 2 imposing Norman towers of c. 1170 with, below, evocative foundations of *church* (17) built in 669 by Bassa, St Augustine's follower (demolished as recently as 1809 for no good reason). Saxon cross (20, 21) found here now in Canterbury crypt.

Repton, Derbyshire. *St Wystan,* major survival of capital of Anglo-Saxon kingdom of Mercia. Crypt with walls perhaps as early as c. 760, spiral columns and dome vaults, c. 840, burial place of kings Aethelbald (d.757) and Wiglaf (d.840). Of church above crypt, chancel, E side of crossing, part of N transept are now thought to be Mercian, c. 840–70 (by Taylor, earlier scholars thought early C11). (See also under Tamworth and Chapter 1 re Mercia.)

Restenneth, Tayside Region. *Priory church* (39), just outside Forfar to E. Tall square tower, lower part attributed to c. 710 (to the baptised King Nechtan of Pictdom) but stylistically of c. 1040, upper part, c. 1100, spire C15. Church itself rebuilt in 1100s and later.

Restormel Castle, N of Lostwithiel, Cornwall. Excellent shell-keep (45) in high remote position, round walls, c. 1200, stone buildings within are later.

Rhossili (or Rhosili), West Glamorgan. Norman *church* largely rebuilt, but traces include handsome doorway and setting is tremendous.

Richmond, North Yorkshire. *Castle* (45), major Norman example, started in 1071, for its separate stone Scolland's Hall (83) (roofless walls of its lower storey, plus solar and Hall itself on 1st floor with windows, surviving) and some curtain walls (all this of c. 1090). Lower 2 storeys of keep of c. 1090 too (then gatehouse), but keep itself (48) splendid rectangular work of c. 1150–80, well preserved. *St Mary* has Norman traces, mostly later. *St Martin's Priory,* by railway station, ruins of Benedictine monastery – low tower and Norman doorway.

Rievaulx Abbey, North Yorkshire. (103, 125.) Cistercian, founded c. 1131 (see Chapter 5), very early pointed arcades and aisle vaults, c. 1140 (see under Durham and Fountains), as are transepts. Fine ruins include cloister, c. 1180, and parts of chapter house, treasury and its undercroft, warming house, infirmary, abbot's lodging and reredorter, all of c. 1180–1200 and with waterleaf capitals and other Cistercian motifs; the rest (including refectory, lavatorium, and external chapel) C13.

Ripley, Surrey. *Church,* with fine Norman chancel, much ornamented, of c. 1160. Nave now by B. Ferrey, 1846.

Ripon, North Yorkshire. *Cathedral* (20), Benedictine monastery founded by St Wilfrid in c. 670 (see Chapter 1 and under Hexham) destroyed in 950, but famous crypt of c. 670 (for pilgrims venerating saints' bones brought from Rome by Wilfrid) is intact, impressive small chambers of iron-hard cement over stone. Canonical church started in c. 1170–1200, chancel of that date Transitional, crossing mixed; the rest later. Chapter house, c. 1200, but chapel beneath it much earlier, perhaps c. 1100.

Ripple, Hereford and Worcester. *Church* and tower Transitional, perhaps 1190–1230, with later work too.

Rochester, Kent. *Cathedral* (95, 123, 177), Gundulf's Tower by N transept remains of 1077–1108 work, and part of crypt. Notable work of c. 1150 in W portal and front, with less satisfactory Norman nave. Anglo-Saxon carving in crypt. *Monastic buildings*: E side of cloister, entry to chapter house, doorway to dormitory, all of c. 1120–40. *Castle* (48, 49, 52), tremendous keep built in 1127 by William of Corbeuil, Archbishop of Canterbury. Forebuilding contains entrance and chapel above. Keep lacks floors now, but impressive interiors. Hall in 3rd and 4th storeys, 2 solars (private rooms) above it.

Rock, Hereford and Worcester. Very ambitious *church,* basically of c. 1170, ornamented with 3-dimensional zigzag, battlement motif, etc. Rich N doorway and chancel arch may be late work by sculptor who decorated Shobdon (q.v.) and Kilpeck (q.v.).

Rodmell, East Sussex. Strange little *church,* c. 1200, with late Norman and early Gothic mixed confusingly.
Romsey, Hampshire. *Abbey church (95, 117, 120),* one of the loveliest of all Norman Romanesque buildings. Nunnery was founded in c. 970, its vanished buildings now witnessed only by Saxon sculpture of Rood and of Crucifixion. Norman abbey church, built in c. 1120–1200 (E end rebuilt later), its nave, crossing and transepts forming soaring space and finely detailed.
Rothbury, Northumberland. At All Saints Church, the *Rothbury Cross,* c. 800 (or rather its lower shaft forming font support – the rest of it in Black Gate Museum, Newcastle Castle).
Rudford, Gloucestershire. Good early Norman *church,* c. 1120, nave and vaulted chancel, E window and chancel arch zigzagged.
Ruthwell, Dumfries and Galloway Region. Famous sculpted stone *cross (23)* of c. 700 stands in special viewing room in Ruthwell church (key from a nearby cottage). Complete with its head, cross has the most accomplished relief sculpture of its period in Europe (see also

Rochester cathedral, Kent. Detail of the west front, with elongated blank arcading and other carved ornament of c. 1140–50

its sister, but shaft only, at Bewcastle, q.v., over the Border).
Ryton-on-Dunsmore, Warwickshire. *Church,* early Norman nave and chancel, c. 1090, roll-moulded windows, doors, etc. Tower C14 and several later windows.
St Albans, Hertfordshire. *Cathedral (27, 95, 110, 111, 112),* no remains of King Offa of Mercia's C8 abbey on site of first British martyrdom, except perhaps the baluster-shafts re-used in Norman transept's gallery apertures. Benedictine abbey church (cathedral since C19) is the most complete early Norman major cathedral in Britain. Central tower, crossing with tall arches, transepts and E part of lengthy nave are all of 1077–88 – of flint and re-used Roman bricks from nearby Verulamium. No decorative carving (though some abstract patterns painted around arches), dramatic contrasts of fierce solids with voids, surfaces whitewashed. Later Norman doorway and blank arcading in transept. W end nave and E end chancel C13, etc. No remains of Norman monastic buildings outside. *St Michael,* St Michael's Street, nave and chancel walls are Anglo-Saxon, c. 950, with some surviving windows. Norman aisles, c. 1110, but nave heightened and other changes later.
St Aldhelm's Chapel, St Aldhelm's Head, Dorset. Remote chapel on headland S of Corfe. Square plan on tiny scale, with central pier and rib-vaults, c. 1180, so unusual a form for its time that one wonders about its original purpose.
St Andrews, Fife Region. Northern outpost of Northumbrian kingdom in C8. Enormous *cathedral (124)* of 1160–1318 now a series of dramatic fragments of high walls, mostly Norman Romanesque, and monastic ruins (abandoned after Reformation). *St Rule's Church* (or St Regulus) *(40, 67, 69),* beside cathedral, still has complete tall square tower, chancel walls and outline of nave gable (built c. 1140, probably as 1st cathedral, but tower appears earlier). *Museum* contains many Northumbrian school C8–10 finely carved cross stones, etc., including famous figure-sculpted St Andrews Sarcophagus, C8, showing lively scenes of David the hunter and shepherd.
St Bees, Cumbria. Almost complete

church of c. 1160, formerly that of Benedictine nunnery founded in 650 and again in c. 1120. Splendid 3-order doorway, zigzag, figures and some beakhead. Chancel Transitional, c. 1190, with lancets and waterleaf capitals. Restored by Butterfield, 1855.

St Breward, Cornwall. By Bodmin Moor. *Church* has irregular aisled Norman nave, crudely carved capitals.

St Briavels, Gloucestershire. Remote in SW of county, *church* has fine quite early Norman nave arcade and late Norman crossing.

St Clears, Dyfed. Attractive *church* (65, 66) with long dark Norman nave and large, now distorted, plumply roll-moulded chancel arch, c. 1110–20.

St Clement, near Truro, Cornwall. *Cross*, probably C7, in churchyard, with Latin and Celtic script (Ogham).

St Cross, Hampshire. See under Winchester.

St Cross South Elmham, Suffolk. See under South Elmham.

St David's, Dyfed. *Cathedral* (75, 125, 179), on site of monastery (94) founded by St David in late 500s. Norman building started in 1176 with chancel and crossing (destroyed by fire and rebuilt Gothic). Nave of c. 1190–1200 survives, with capitals and zigzag, etc., ornament in arcades taking extraordinary tubular late forms. W front neo-Norman (based on ruined fragments) by Sir G. Scott, timber roof also Victorian, both reasonably well done. *Bishop's Palace*, over stream from cathedral, tremendous affair, mostly C13 but dramatic C12 undercroft to 1 range, with shallow tunnel-vault.

St Germans, Cornwall. Once an Anglo-Saxon cathedral (no traces), severe *church* was that of Augustinian priory. 2 bays of early Norman nave and spaces under W towers, W front late Norman but plain, 7-order doorway with zigzag, parts of towers; rest of church Gothic.

St Kew, near Wadebridge, Cornwall. At church, inscribed *stone*, probably C7, in Ogham (Celtic script) and Latin.

St Martin-by-Looe, near East Looe, Cornwall. *Church* has N door of c. 1130 and Norman font.

St Ninian's Cave, Dumfries and Galloway Region. SW of Whithorn, near Glasserton, a minor road goes to Physgill House. 1 mile's walk to seashore and the cave is to the left. Holy place since St Ninian's time, cave has had several

floors, and there are some roughly inscribed crosses on walls.

St Piran-in-Sabulo, S of Newquay, Cornwall. In sand-dune country, preserved stone and clay walls of small chapel of *St Piran* (a missionary from Ireland), dating from between 500 and 700, in modern shelter, having been engulfed in sand in about 1000. Inland, dunes covered later church too, but simple *cross* stands.

Saltford, Avon. *Saltford Manor* (82, 82), in centre of Saltford, small village E of Keynsham. Manor-house of c. 1150, garden front still retains ornate 2-light round-arched window of 1st-floor hall, as well as basic tall shape. Much Norman masonry and gable details (other windows and roof later). Inside, some simple Norman stone arches and windows, though hall sub-compartmented and other rooms rearranged when C17 extension added to main front. (Private house, no visitors unless arranged by letter with proprietor.)

Sancreed, near Penzance, Cornwall. In village churchyard, 2 ornate figure-carved *crosses* of 900s.

Sandbach, Cheshire. In Market Place, 2 magnificent carved *crosses* (23) of c. 850 (1 has part of its cross-head still) on step-pyramidal bases.

Sandwich, Kent. *St Mary*, Norman tower fell in 1668, leaving a shadow of former church. *St Clement*, fine Norman tower remains upright.

Sarratt, Hertfordshire. Small Norman *church*, its plan a Greek (equal-armed) cross. Crossing arches survive, though chancel elongated later and other changes.

Scarborough, North Yorkshire. *Castle* on headland, keep (48) of c. 1160–70 and curtain walls.

Seaton Delaval, Northumberland. Small and pretty Norman *church*, c. 1140, enlarged later, chancel arch zigzagged and roll-moulded.

Selby, North Yorkshire. *Abbey* (115) (Benedictine), founded c. 1070, transepts, c. 1100, arcades of nave, c. 1120–40, with incised drum-piers and zigzag (Durham-style) but gallery above of c. 1180 and later, chancel (replacing Norman one), c. 1300 Decorated Gothic. Monastic buildings disappeared.

Selham, West Sussex. Fascinating earliest Norman *church* (61), c. 1070s, nave and chancel, with evidence of Saxon

Detail of the Norman nave, St David's cathedral, Dyfed, South Wales (c. 1190–8). Spatially rather bland, but the now old-fashioned zigzag carved ornament is developed into strange tubular forms

masons at work in carved ornament.

Sempringham, Lincolnshire. Notable as origin of St Gilbert of Sempringham's Gilbertine Order (for monks and nuns in different buildings, sharing a church divided along its central line). Abbey church vanished, but *parish church* has exciting Norman carving, c. 1160, in corbel-table and doorways, nave and windows.

Sherborne, Dorset. Abbey church was seat of bishops of Wessex and Saxon wall and door visible at W end. Tall crossing arches and transepts, c. 1120, of Norman Benedictine *abbey church* partly survive, with ornate S porch, c. 1170; the rest glorious later Gothic. *Monastery,* various

fragments in school, the best the chapel undercroft (now boys' library reading room). *Castle,* outside town (near Sir Walter Raleigh's Sherborne Castle of 1590s), built by Bishop of Salisbury in 1107–35, remains include Norman gatehouse, shattered keep, chapel walls and hall in ruins with fragments of intersecting arcading and zigzagged windows, around court.

Sherston, Wiltshire. *Church* with good zigzagged nave arcade of c. 1160 and relics of unnamed Norman saint, ill-treated these days.

Shipley, West Sussex. Complete Norman *church,* c. 1125 or earlier, built by the Knights Templar. Nave, tower and

179

chancel, with very interesting carving. Aisle added by J. L. Pearson, 1893.

Shobdon, Hereford and Worcester. Earliest c. 1145 *carvings* of hypothetical so-called Shobdon master were saved from ruined church and can be seen (very eroded) in folly called Shobdon Arches in grounds of now-demolished house, Shobdon Court. His attributed later work, among the finest Norman sculpture in the country (with almost Celtic flavour to the interlaced work, etc.), can be seen at churches of c. 1150–80 at (in possible chronological order) Kilpeck, Fownhope, Brinsop, Stretton Sugwas, Rock, perhaps Rowlstone, Chaddesley Corbett (all Hereford and Worcester), Ruardean (Gloucestershire) and Much Wenlock (Shropshire). *Font* at Castle Frome may also be by him or a pupil.

Shoreham, West Sussex. Old Shoreham: N wall of *church* Saxon with blocked doorway, c. 900, lovely Norman crossing, transepts, central tower and nave, c. 1140. Carved capitals, rosettes and zigzag plus billet motif in ornate arches. Chancel and other alterations C14, and restored with some neo-Norman work by J. M. Neale, 1839. New Shoreham: *church* (76), major Norman building, imposing tower and transepts (nave largely destroyed) c. 1130, then in c. 1180–90 the elaborately carved chancel with much inventive foliage, etc., some pointed arches, in Transitional style close to the early Gothic of contemporary choir of Canterbury cathedral (q.v.).

Shrewsbury, Shropshire. *Castle* of 1164, walls survive beside river. *St Mary*, St Mary's Place, has transepts and W tower, with S porch of c. 1170–1200.

Sidbury, Devon. *Church* has Anglo-Saxon crypt and carved slab of c. 1000, W tower, c. 1180, with corbelled rib-vaulting at bottom inside, some Norman windows and other detail, and Transitional nave arcade, c. 1200; the rest of this splendid church is Gothic.

Sinnington, North Yorkshire. Barn beside church to N was 1st-floor *manor hall*, c. 1190, 1 Norman window; the rest C15.

Skenfrith, Gwent. *Castle* in village guarding river has large round keep (55), c. 1200 (like Pembroke, q.v.) on earlier motte, spiral stairs in rounded turrets (all floorless now), plus curtain wall and

towers (rebuilt rounded later) on trapezoidal plan, also fairly ruined.

Skipwith, North Yorkshire. On border with Humberside, *church* has Anglo-Saxon W tower and excellent tower arch, c. 1040 (added to lower tower, which was earlier a W porch).

Slough, Buckinghamshire. *St Laurence*, Upton, now suburb of Slough. Almost complete and excellent Norman church. Norman nave (S aisle Victorian), central tower space and rib-vaulted chancel, c. 1140.

Smeeth, Kent. Massive *parish church*, nave and chancel, c. 1120, aisle and chapel, c. 1200.

Snodhill Castle. See under Peterchurch.

Sompting, West Sussex. *Church* (40, 41, *41*, 42), among the most famous of Anglo-Saxon churches for its 'Rhenish Helm' steeple, c. 1040–60, only surviving example in England of type perhaps widespread. Inside, off-centre tower arch (for altar in tower?), interesting Saxon (and later) sculpture, and mystifying series of spaces formed by fine Norman work by the Knights Templar, c. 1130 onwards.

Sookholme, Nottinghamshire. Like Littleborough (q.v.), tiny pre-1100 Norman *church*, well-preserved, nave, chancel arch and chancel, some windows Gothicised.

Southampton, Hampshire. Best approach to unique Norman remains is along the old town walls now facing one stretch of Western Esplanade road (in C12 this was town quay). One stretch of *town wall* (87, *87*) (below site of now-destroyed castle) dates from c. 1190, with flat buttresses and castle vaulted cellar behind wall. Further S, section of C14 wall called 'The Arcade' includes (beside gateway) stone 2-storey *Merchant's House* (*86*, 87), c. 1150, with round-arched doorway and 2-light windows (interior largely destroyed, but can be visited through Tudor House Museum behind it). Further S still, in Porter Lane, is ruined *Long House* (87), c. 1180 (sometimes misleadingly called Canute's Palace), again 2-storey. *St Michael*, St Michael's Square, has lower part of early Norman crossing tower (rest of church later). *St Julian*, Winkle Street, has memorable Transitional pointed roll-moulded chancel arch, c. 1190, with strangely carved capitals.

South Elmham St Cross, Suffolk. Ruin

of c. 950 *'Minster' church*, magically sited in wood ½ mile SW of parish church. Walls survive of W *narthex* or ante-chamber, aisleless nave and traces of vanished apse.

Southend-on-Sea, Essex. *Prittlewell Priory* (Benedictine), in Priory Park. W range and refectory of c. 1170 survive as Southend Museum. *South Shoebury church*, now in Southend suburb, has Norman doorways, nave, chancel and chancel arch, c. 1140.

Southwell, Nottinghamshire. The *Minster* (117, *121*) is one of the glories of Norman architecture on a grand scale, on site of more ancient building (1 Anglo-Saxon tympanum survives). Norman collegiate church, founded c. 1108 (its 1st chancel replaced C13), 8-bay nave, transepts and crossing, c. 1120–50, tall crossing arch with cable-pattern moulding, nave with low drum-piers and gallery of unusual proportions. E crossing piers have primitively sculpted capitals. Exterior – from W all that one sees (except large W C15 window) is Norman. W towers with pyramidal roofs, nave, transepts, handsome porch and central tower (though some parts have had to be rebuilt). This church and its canons owned a quarter of all Nottinghamshire before Reformation.

Sproxton, Leicestershire. In churchyard, *cross* of c. 950 is complete, but carving much worn.

Stafford. *St Chad*, Greengate Street, has Norman nave, crossing and chancel. Much restoration by Sir G. Scott in 1870s.

Stanton Lacy, Shropshire. N transept and nave walls of *church*, c. 1050, plus some Norman and much C14 work.

Stanton St Quintin, Wiltshire. *Church* with handsome central tower and tower arch, c. 1120.

Stapleford, Nottinghamshire. *Cross*, c. 1020–40, in churchyard, with figures and interlace.

Stapleford, Wiltshire. *Church*, nave has tremendous Norman drum-piers of c. 1120, scalloped capitals and square abaci, but with projecting zigzag and even dog-tooth of c. 1190–1200 above; the rest Gothic.

Steetly, Derbyshire. Tiny *church* of c. 1100, aisleless nave, chancel and apse. 4-order S doorway, c. 1150, with zigzag and beakhead. Chancel arch, 4-order, with sculpted capitals and zigzag plus

battlement motif, etc. Apse arch and vaulting roll-moulded plus billet motif.

Stewkley, Buckinghamshire. Glorious complete middle-sized Norman *church* (*9, 51, 76*) of c. 1140–50. W front with dragon tympanum. Nave, central tower space and vaulted square-ended chancel. Rich zigzag carving everywhere and beakhead, etc., on imposing tower arch and chancel arch. Classic example, eschewing originality of motif.

Steyning, West Sussex. Major Norman *church* (*75*) for excellent nave with carved ornament, c. 1160–80, sculpted heads, rosettes, zigzag and even dog-tooth, with drum-piers and clerestory above. Tower arches, c. 1170, with early zigzag. Chancel is a Victorian blunder by G. M. Hills, 1863.

Stogursey, Somerset. Striking *church*, crossing splendidly c. 1100, Norman arcade and vaulted chancel, c. 1180.

Stoke-sub-Hamdon, Somerset. Enjoyable *church* (*65, 66, 74*) with wild early Norman tympanum (zodiac animals), notable zigzag and lozenge chancel arch, c. 1130–40, impressive vaulted crossing space, c. 1180, Transitional.

Stone, Buckinghamshire. *Church* has Norman S doorway and N arcade, c. 1130. Famous font with dramatic carved scene of man and dove fighting a monster eating another man.

Stonegrave, North Yorkshire. *Church*, with tower and simple nave arcades, but with waterleaf so c. 1170; the rest C19. Excellent cross of 900s, and Norse carved slab with archer and dragon.

Stoneleigh, Warwickshire. *St Mary*, large Norman work, N doorway with reel-pattern and self-destructive dragons in tympanum, c. 1120–30. Broad nave and ornately zigzagged and sculpted chancel arch, chancel with zigzag arcading, good font. *Stoneleigh Abbey* has many Norman fragments, c. 1160–1200 (Cistercian), among ruins around famous Georgian mansion.

Stopham, West Sussex. Imposing village *church* (*61*) with nave and chancel just post-Conquest, perhaps 1070s. Apse removed.

Stottesdon, Shropshire. *Church* has tympanum and lintel of c. 1060–70, early Norman tower, font and N arcade of nave, c. 1160.

Stoughton, West Sussex. *Church* is basically 1080s cruciform, with massive chancel arch and many late Norman windows, etc.

Stow, Lincolnshire. Huge *church* (*33, 34*) for Anglo-Saxon times, the largest to survive. Built by one of two bishops called Eadnoth, so either c. 1010 or c. 1040. Spacious cruciform plan, major rounded Anglo-Saxon crossing arches (now reinforced by later pointed arches inserted inside the crossing space), long nave, high transepts with Anglo-Saxon doorways, etc. Chancel rebuilt by Normans, in ruins by C19, rebuilt perhaps exaggeratedly by J. L. Pearson in 1850s.

Strata Florida, Dyfed. Ruined Cistercian abbey, lovely setting in the hills N of Pontrhydfendigaid. Built by Rhys ap Gruffydd from 1184 onwards, low walls only remain, except for 1 famous enriched late Norman doorway.

Strethall, Essex. *Church* with Saxon nave and chancel arch, c. 1060. Tower and chancel C15.

Stretton Sugwas, Hereford and Worcester. Victorian *church*, but incorporating Norman S doorway and fine tympanum (Samson riding the Lion) of Shobdon (q.v.) style, c. 1150–60.

Studland, Dorset. *Church* (*63, 64*), a little isolated from the village, is a classic early Norman work. Nave, tower space and square-ended chancel. Nave, c. 1090, E parts rib-vaulted so c. 1120 or slightly later. Arches with plump roll-mouldings, shallow carving on capitals. Outside, these forms are stated, though top of tower never built, with slightly set-off (i.e. stepped, very unusual in Norman times) buttresses and wild corbel-table faces on both sides. E window altered, but spatially both stimulating and serene.

Sulgrave, Northamptonshire. *Castle*, W of church, has Norman remains but also rare traces of an Anglo-Saxon lord's dwelling, c. 1020. Excavations have revealed 80-ft-long wooden hall, with separate wooden kitchen and small stone building whose walls survive. *Church* has 1 Anglo-Saxon doorway in tower.

Sunderland (Monkwearmouth), Tyne and Wear. *St Peter* (*18*), Monkwearmouth, stands in industrial centre of Sunderland, on a green which was the site of the monastery (18) founded (like Jarrow, q.v.) by St Benedict Biscop from Canterbury in c. 675. Lower part of tower is of that date, an extraordinary survival originally

a porch with turned baluster-shafts typical of the time and some eroded sculpture. Upper tower, c. 1000. Inside, W wall of tall Anglo-Saxon nave can be seen; the rest C14 and C19, rescuing it from ruin.

Sutton, Kent. Nice little Norman *church* of nave, chancel and quasi-apse.

Sutton Bingham, Somerset. Small simple early Norman *church* of aisleless nave and chancel, ornate chancel arch added in c. 1160, windows and wall-paintings later medieval.

Sutton Courtenay, Oxfordshire. House called *Norman Hall*, W of church (which has Norman zigzag features, etc.), is a manor-house of c. 1200. Plain stone, fine Transitional doorways with dog-tooth, etc., carving, some later windows and alterations, good timber roof.

Sutton Valence, Kent. Small overgrown *tower keep*, E of village, wall up to 1st-floor level survives.

Swaffham Prior, Cambridgeshire. Gothic *church*, with notable Norman tower – square at bottom, octagonal above.

Swyncombe, Oxfordshire. Small early Norman *church* of c. 1080, nave and apsed chancel. Altered by B. Ferrey, 1850.

Tamworth, Staffordshire. Offa, the great king of Mercia (see Chapter 1), had his palace at Tamworth, and Alfred's formidable daughter Aethelfleda later made the town a fortified *burh* like those of her father. *Castle*, shell-keep of c. 1180 and herringbone wall of c. 1080 remain of Norman castle perhaps on palace site, but many later buildings too. (See also under Repton re Mercia.)

Tarrington, Hereford and Worcester. Norman *church* with nave and chancel of c. 1130, apse destroyed.

Tasburgh, Norfolk. *Church*, with fine Anglo-Danish round tower with blank arcading, c. 1020–60; church itself Gothic.

Tewkesbury, Gloucestershire. *Abbey* (*115, 117*), one of the great Norman Benedictine abbey churches, built from 1087 onwards. W front, c. 1150, survives with Gothic window inserted. Inside, chancel rebuilt later, but there are parts of transepts, the entire crossing and the whole nave of c. 1100–21, with amazingly high drum-piers, like Gloucester cathedral (q.v.). Roof vaulting post-Norman.

Thetford, Norfolk. Benedictine *abbey*

church of c. 1107–40 is in ruins: scant remains of apsed chancel with radiating chapels, nave and crossing, remnants of Norman cloister, chapter house, etc. *Other monasteries*: even slighter remains of a nunnery and an Augustinian priory can be seen. *Other remains*: Thetford has been the site of some of the most important excavations of pre-Norman domestic foundations – Anglian huts of c. 600 and Anglo-Danish houses of c. 900. The help of local archaeologists should be sought for information.

Thockrington, Northumberland. Small solitary early Norman *church* high beside farm, with tunnel-vaulted chancel and plain chancel arch, though windows altered.

Thorington, Suffolk. *Church*, with one of about 40 round church towers in Suffolk (there are even more in Norfolk) of Anglo-Saxon or Norman dates. Good late Anglo-Danish example, c. 1050, with bell-openings and band of blank arcading of that date. Church itself Victorian.

Thorney, Cambridgeshire. Part of nave of the Benedictine abbey of c. 1100–8 survives in present *church*, with altered W front and neo-Norman E parts by E. Blore, 1840.

Thorpe Salvin, South Yorkshire. *Church* has much Norman work of c. 1150–80 – nave arcades, chancel arch, etc. – mixing earlier and late motifs in good carving. Some windows and chancel Gothic. In Laughton-en-le-Morthen, about 2 miles N of Thorpe Salvin, *church* with Anglo-Saxon N doorway, N arcade and some windows late Norman, lovely spire Gothic.

Thorpe-next-Haddiscoe, Norfolk. *Church*, with round Anglo-Danish tower (unusual stonework at bottom), its windows carved from single stones, blank arcading. Nave of church and bell-openings of tower are latest Anglian or earliest Norman. Victorian chancel.

Tickencote, Leicestershire. Richly ornamented small Norman *church*, nave-plus-chancel. Gothicised C15, then re-Normanised by S. P. Cockerell in 1792. Chancel has decorated exterior, c. 1130, zigzag and billet. Chancel arch 4-order, zigzagged, beakheaded, relief figure-sculpted, etc., 1160–70, and ornate rib-vaulted chancel.

Tickhill, South Yorkshire. *Castle* has gatehouse, c. 1140 (outer side refaced C15), and curtain walls, c. 1180 – the

only Norman buildings left around high motte of Henry II's vanished polygonal (10-sided) shell-keep of 1178.

Tilney All Saints, Norfolk. *Church* nave and chancel form a continuous space of c. 1180–90. Roof and tower later.

Ting Holm, near Scalloway, Shetland. Little *amphitheatre*, on promontory (formerly an island) on Loch of Tinwall, was the *Ting* or *Alting* (folk parliament) of the Shetland Norse. Walled enclosure and the hollowed annual gathering place of C9–11 survive, but the stone seats were smashed in C18.

Tintagel, Cornwall. High on inshore side of headland, Norman *castle* (45) ruins of c. 1145 by Henry I's illegitimate son, Duke of Cornwall, consisting of shattered gatehouse and Hall, with chapel above. On outer headland, beyond later parts of castle, extensive *Celtic monastery* remains of cells and other buildings (lower walls only now). Remote from village and castle, *church*, largely of Norman masonry, but few features unaltered.

Titchfield, Hampshire. *Church* (27) has notable early Saxon porch, c. 800, now lower part of tower, with Norman work in interior.

Tixover, Leicestershire. *Church*, SW outside village, a short walk. Powerful tower arch, c. 1120–30, S door and S arcade, c. 1180 with waterleaf capitals and c. 1200 with pointed arches and stiff-leaf, some windows Gothicised.

Tomen y Rodwydd, Clwyd. Also called Castell yr Adwy, or Ial, 1 mile SW of Llandegla, or 8 miles N of Llangollen, near A525. No buildings here, but classic earthwork *motte and bailey* built by the Welsh as late as 1149.

Torpenhow, Cumbria. *Church* has fierce zigzagging on doorway and chancel arch with other motifs, c. 1160–70, but a provincial rendering. Nave arcades and chancel of same period, several windows altered later.

Totnes, Devon. *Castle* (*44*, *45*), very attractive park-like bailey earthworks and high motte of c. 1100, with stone shell-keep of c. 1200 around its top.

Tredunnock, Gwent. *Church* has early Norman chancel, somewhat altered.

Tretower, Powys. Confusing *castle* remains of shell-keep and other work of c. 1150, with enlargement of c. 1230, in the town.

Tutbury, Staffordshire. *Castle*, on hill

above town and river, was stronghold of de Ferrers family, some of William I's major barons and grantees of estates all over England (see Chapter 2), later earls of Derby. Of their castle, only ruined chapel, nave and chancel, c. 1120, survive; the rest mostly C15. *Parish church*, below castle but above town, is much grander. Nave, c. 1130, W front and S doorway, c. 1160, with complex beakhead, zigzag, etc. Chancel by G. E. Street, 1866.

Twywell, Northamptonshire. Small Norman *church* with ornate carving, though partly remodelled later.

Tynemouth, Tyne and Wear. C7 foundation, ruins are of the *church* of Benedictine priory of c. 1090–1130, some Norman work (e.g. reredorter) among generally later monastery.

Tynninghame, Lothian Region. *Old parish church* is a roofless ruined fragment of glorious Norman work of c. 1160 (now in grounds of Tynninghame House) on site of C9 monastery. Among ruins, ornate chancel and apse arched with zigzag, billet and lozenge motifs. Capitals scalloped, voluted or fish-scale motif. Traces of rib-vaulting here. Little remains of nave or tower.

Tywyn, Gwynedd. Site of monastic *clas* founded in 500s by St Cadfan. Collegiate *church*, large and cruciform, started in c. 1150. Norman arcaded nave survives (round clerestory windows); the rest Victorian and not well done.

Usk, Gwent. *Castle*, on town hilltop, with small rectangular Norman keep, plus later towers and walls (private, but open sometimes). *Church* in Priory Street, tower and nave originally Norman, c. 1140, but mostly altered.

Wallingford, Oxfordshire. *St Leonard* has fine apse and chancel, arches with early c. 1120–30 carving, but Victorian neo-Norman work too.

Walmer, Kent. *Walmer Court*, beside old churchyard, has battered shell of a small fortified house in its grounds.

Walsoken, Norfolk. Magnificent *church*, near Wisbech, Norman arcaded nave and chancel, c. 1180–90, chancel arch zigzagged but pointed. Tower, etc., later.

Waltham Holy Cross, Essex. *Waltham Abbey* (99, 115), its church on site of (later King) Harold's abbey of c. 1060. Norman nave, c. 1120, survives, tremendous design with Durham-type drum-piers (incised with spirals, etc.),

gallery and clerestory above. Restored in 1859 by William Burges (who also built E end to seal it off) from ruined state following Dissolution of Monasteries in 1530s.

Warblington, Hampshire. *Church*, Saxon tower with door-openings high in walls, nave late Norman.

Warden, Northumberland. *Church* has Anglian tower, c. 1050, with low tower arch inside.

Wareham, Dorset. *St Mary*, scant traces of former major Anglo-Saxon church, except 5 inscribed stones of 600–900, sunken Norman chapel off chancel and Norman lead font among later medieval and Victorian rebuilding. *St Martin* was also Anglo-Saxon (late) and retains chancel arch, 1 chancel window, long-and-short work quoins outside, as well as late Norman nave arcade and traces of C12 wall-painting.

Warkworth, Northumberland. Intact fairly large Norman *church*, long nave with its original c. 1100 windows on N side, chancel splendidly rib-vaulted with zigzagging, c. 1130–40, tower, c. 1200. *Castle*, ruins of Norman Great Hall, c. 1200, survive, also gatehouse and postern towers at W (keep as late as c. 1400).

Warndon, Hereford and Worcester. Timber porch of *church* may be pre-1200, exceptionally early for a projecting porch (rather than portico).

Warnford, Hampshire. Interesting Transitional-style *church*, strong tower of c. 1180, nave and chancel, c. 1200, with lancet windows.

Warwick, Cumbria. *Church*, largely Victorian, but tower arch of c. 1130 and notable for its preserved apse with unique external round-headed lancet blank arcading all round – very powerful effect (difficult to date, perhaps c. 1180–90).

Water Stratford, Buckinghamshire. Simple little village *church*, Norman tower with pyramid roof, doorways with sculpted tympana (one of Christ enthroned, the other a wild dragon), windows all post-Norman.

Waythe, Lincolnshire. Victorian *church* at E and W ends, but has Anglo-Saxon central tower, c. 1040.

Weaverthorpe, Humberside. *Church* (67, *68*) has tall fierce tower, c. 1110, contemporary nave and chancel (many windows altered), restored and roofed by

G. E. Street, 1872.

Wells, Somerset. Present *cathedral* was started in c. 1180, within Norman period, but is essentially C13 Gothic.

West Malling, Kent. W front of *Malling Abbey* (82), as well as shell of a small c. 1150 *house* (82) (zigzagged windows) behind shop in High Street, and small Norman keep, *St Leonard's Tower*, survive.

West Woolfardisworthy (pronounced Woolsery), Devon. *Church* has 3-order arched S doorway, c. 1150 beakhead and zigzag (Shebbear and Buckland Brewer not far away have similar doors, presumably the work of one local or travelling craftsman), Norman S transept and simple font; the rest later.

Westdean, East Sussex. *Charleston Manor* (82), ½ mile NW of village, has well-preserved house of c. 1200 as its S wing. Hall on upper level, 2-light ornate round-arched window at one end, lancet at other. (Private, write to proprietor for permission to visit.)

Westness, Rousay Island, Orkney. Good example of Norse settler's *cairn grave*, c. 850, which contained a finely dressed woman.

Weston, Hertfordshire. *Church,* early Norman crossing and transept survive, nave and chancel later.

Whalley, Lancashire. In St Mary's churchyard, 3 Anglo-Saxon (Northumbrian) *crosses*, one very fine, C10 or C11 flowing spirals, etc.

Whaplode, Lincolnshire. *Church* with good Norman interior, nave and zigzagged chancel arch.

Whissonsett, Norfolk. At St Mary's, the notable *Whissonsett Cross* of perhaps c. 900. Interlaced shaft, cross-head within circle.

Whitby, North Yorkshire. Evocative and historic Anglo-Saxon place, though ruins are largely post-Norman. Celtic monastery was founded in 657; in 664 the Synod (church conference) was held here which decided that Roman ritual, rather than the Celtic Church, would be supreme in England – excavations have shown a long building and several oblong huts, and Norman *abbey church* of c. 1090. On high hillside above the sea now are abbey ruins C13 and delectable *parish church* with Norman tower (altered), S doorway within porch, window, corbel-table, nave buttresses, chancel, chancel arch, c. 1150, and tower

arch, c. 1190, almost lost among gorgeous C18 alterations and furnishings.

White Castle, Gwent. E of Abergavenny and 1 mile E of Llanvetherine village. Rectangular keep, c. 1150 (foundations only preserved), curtain wall, 1185, circular wall-towers added C13 when keep demolished, outer ward later still.

Whithorn, Dumfries and Galloway Region. Under E end of present C13 priory church ruins, burials and a simple stone chapel have been excavated (not visible now) that may be the lower walls of the *Casa Candida* (13) (White House or Chapel) built in c. 400 by St Ninian, a Christian missionary to the Southern Picts from late-Roman England. Museum has major collection of *crosses* and inscribed *stones* dating from c. 450 (Latin inscription) to Ogham script of c. 600 and Northumbrian interlace of c. 800–900.

Whittingham, Northumberland. *Church,* lower part of tower and quoins of nave are Anglian, c. 1000.

Wickham, Berkshire. Victorian *church,* but W tower late Anglo-Saxon, c. 1020, long-and-short work quoins, single-splay windows, double bell-openings with stumpy columns in middle of wall; top altered.

Wimborne Minster, Dorset. (125.) Church of a house of secular Canons, started in c. 1135–40, the crossing and nave of c. 1170 and Transitional, with zigzagged pointed arcades and round-arched gallery above. Major church, rather messed up by later centuries.

Winchester, Hampshire. The capital of Alfred and his Wessex dynasty of kings of England. Foundations of 3 Saxon cathedrals or major churches have been excavated, but only one piece of Saxon sculpted frieze survives. Norman *cathedral* (95, *111,* 112), started in 1070. Groin-vaulted crypt, c. 1070–80, and severely beautiful N and S transepts of c. 1090 survive (the rest rebuilt Gothic), together with entrance arches to chapter house. *Wolvesey Palace* (for the bishop) exists in ruins beside present Bishop's Palace (83) – walls of keep, tower and one range of c. 1140, plus roofless Great Hall, c. 1170 (not open to the public). *St Cross* (126, *126,* 127, *186*) (with later almshouses of its Hospital) is signposted up a suburban side-street from the main road S out of Winchester. Church is amazing – perhaps the finest work of late Norman Transitional architecture. Tall, massive and fierce outside, the high cruciform vaulted interior is elaborately adorned with 3-dimensional zigzag carving of perhaps c. 1190, the arches a mixture of round with early pointed, the whole space intense and moving. Restored by W. Butterfield, C19.

Winchfield, Hampshire. Extraordinary late Norman *church*, with fierce, rather heavy, decoration of c. 1170 – zigzag in 3 dimensions, mouldings in arch soffits, etc., the whole effect almost Moorish.

Windsor, Berkshire. *Castle*, centres on Norman earthen motte of c. 1080, upper Round Tower is of early C19, but around it and lower down are the walls of Henry II's big shell-keep (45) of c. 1180. Norman masonry of that time also survives, e.g. in the Winchester Tower, among extensive later buildings.

Wing, Buckinghamshire. *All Saints* (27, 31, 32, *32*) is a major early and late Anglo-Saxon church. Nave and basic masonry of chancel probably of 700s, the primitive arcades cut through nave walls perhaps rather later. Extensively rebuilt

St Cross Hospital church (c. 1190–1210), Winchester, Hampshire. The transept roof, with the zigzagged ribs of the Norman, transitional to Gothic, vaulting

in c. 950, probably by Lady Aelfgifu, relative of King Eadgar, who built present chancel arch, vaulted crypt under chancel (a crypt of some sort may have already existed) and polygonal E apse, its exterior decorated with lesenes forming blank arcading and triangular-headed blank arcades above (apse interior and windows have been altered). Nave aisles, many windows, etc., rebuilt later.

Wingrave, Buckinghamshire. *Church* has Transitional chancel of c. 1200 with blank arcading and pointed arches, and chamber off chancel with pointed tunnel-vaulting. Nave, etc., later.

Winstone, Gloucestershire. Pretty *church* (63), very simple, tower late Anglo-Saxon, chaste interior (without an E window) early Norman. Or was the whole building Saxon-Norman overlap of 1070s?

Winterborne Tomson, Dorset. In deepest Dorset, N of the Puddles and Bere Regis, but the southmost of the Winterborne villages. Tiny Norman *church* (61, *61*) stands beside manor-house, but otherwise isolated and badly signposted. Classic early Norman one-space church of nave and apse, but unusual for its sheer charm and visible timber frame. Some windows enlarged for daylight, otherwise intact Norman, perhaps of c. 1090.

Winterbourne Steepleton, Dorset. Small *church*, apparently Gothic, but nave masonry and quoins are Anglo-Saxon and, in an external wall, there is a famous relief carving of a flying angel, probably of c. 1000. Also, Norman doorway and window, now disused.

Wirksworth, Derbyshire. Gothic (medieval and Victorian) *church* contains notable sculpted tomb-cover slab, c. 800.

Wisley, Surrey. Little early Norman *church* (61) with belfry, of c. 1100. Simple detail in nave and chancel, unornamented chancel arch.

Witley, Surrey. *Church*, with rare wall-paintings of c. 1180 in Norman nave, chancel Transitional, c. 1200.

Wittering, Cambridgeshire. *Church* has tremendous Anglo-Norse chancel arch, c. 1020, and contemporary corners of nave and chancel. Nave arcade excellent Norman work of c. 1170, with plump roll-mouldings and multiple intersecting zigzag in arches.

Wolverhampton, West Midlands. 14-ft-high Mercian *cross-shaft* of 800s stands

outside St Peter's, the old parish church
in town centre.

Wootton Wawen, Warwickshire.
Church has well-preserved Anglo-Saxon
central tower (top later), with long-and-
short work quoins of c. 1020, tower
space within it, *porticus* openings, etc.,
plus Norman and later rebuildings.

Worcester, Hereford and Worcester.
Cathedral (27, 95), crypt of 1080s is
complete, as is Norman S chancel chapel,
plus a few traces in transepts and nave –
all that remains of the only Norman
cathedral started by an Anglo-Saxon
bishop, Wulstan; the rest C13 and C14.
Monastic buildings: slype (passage from
transept to cloister) is early Norman,
some masonry perhaps Saxon; *chapter
house* (97), c. 1120, is important, for it is
the first to have plan of central pier with
radiating vaults above, later widespread
in England; *refectory undercroft* also
Norman.

Worksop, Nottinghamshire. *Priory
church* (originally Radford Priory),
founded in 1103, Norman W front and
towers, with long c. 1200 nave,
Transitional, alternating round and
octagonal piers, much ornament.
Chancel C20, Lady Chapel fine C13.

Worth, West Sussex. Major late Anglo-
Saxon *church,* c. 1030–50, one of the
largest and most impressive in Britain.
Nave, transepts and apsed chancel (and
their massive arches) form powerful
interior. *Porticus* arches (1 now a door).
Exterior has bold vertical stone lesene-
strips and original nave and apse
windows (2-light, with thick column
between). Spire and W end, etc., later.

Worthing, West Sussex. *Broadwater
church,* N of Worthing town centre,
largely Norman. Brilliantly executed
zigzag, etc., carving, c. 1160, on tower
and chancel, though much restored.

Wroxeter, Shropshire. Was major
Roman town and Roman stones are re-
used in walls of *church.* Tower and
chancel, with its blocked doorway,
c. 1160–80, fine work with zigzag and
Transitional features.

Wroxham, Norfolk. *Church* of mixed
styles, with splendid primitively carved
Norman doorway.

Wyken, West Midlands. In W suburbs
of Coventry. Small simple Norman *parish
church,* c. 1120, almost complete.

Wymondham, Norfolk. *Church* was
that of Benedictine abbey, nave of
c. 1130, which Pope allotted to town's
use in 1249. Towers post-Norman, E end
demolished.

Yarm, Cleveland (Teesside). *Church,*
beside river, away from village centre,
mostly C18 and C19, but preserves
striking Norman W front, with 2 turrets.

York. *Anglian Tower* (8, 18), lower
storey of what is thought to be a stone
tower of c. 630 Northumbria, added to
the older Roman walls NE of the Roman
Multangular Tower, in grounds of St
Mary's Abbey (now public park
containing Yorkshire Museum, where
ring road around the walls crosses River
Ouse). Tower has tunnel-vaulted arches
to its interior and, if it is of that date, is
sole surviving example of Anglo-Saxon
non-ecclesiastical architecture. *St Mary
Bishophill Junior,* Bishophill, important
Anglo-Saxon church. Tower lower part
with Roman brick may be of C8 or C9,
herringbone masonry above and twin
bell-openings, c. 1020–60. Large and
impressive tower arch inside (tower
interior thought to have acted as nave,
see under Barton-on-Humber), simple
c. 1180 nave arcade with round abaci.
Some doors and chancel windows also
seem late Anglian or early Norman. *The
Minster* (75, 100), founded by King
Edwin of Northumbria in 627 in timber,
and stone in c. 650 and later, rebuilt by
Normans from c. 1070 onwards – but
nothing of all that remains except parts of
Norman crypt, which contains fine relief
sculptures of the Virgin and of Hell, both
c. 1130. *St Margaret,* Walmgate, tunnel-
vaulted porch with 3-order ornately
zodiac-carved doorway, c. 1170. *St
Denys,* Walmgate, S doorway, carved
with abstract motifs, c. 1150. *St
Lawrence,* Lawrence Street, outer York to
the E, has S doorway of c. 1170, 3-order,
with animal-carved capitals, medallions,
etc. *St Mary's Abbey* (see Anglian Tower
above) has some Norman out-buildings
among its ruins, and good figure
sculpture from its chapter house is in
museum. *52A Stonegate* (88), behind
modern house, interior walls and 2-light
window of Norman house. *City walls,*
many stretches (especially near gates) are
of Norman masonry, but all gateways
(Bars or 'Bartizans') are C14 or later.

GLOSSARY

Abacus (plural *abaci*). The stone slab between the capital of a pier or column and the arch or wall above that it supports.

Abutment. The wall beside the curve of an arch (see the diagram of an arch on page 10).

Aisle. The long space or spaces running along either side of a nave or chancel, and separated from it by an arcade.

Apse. A semi-circular end of a church or chapel, usually at the east and with an altar in it, derived from Roman early Christian and Byzantine architecture.

Arcade. A row of piers and arches dividing, and opening between, two spaces.

Arcading. A row of arches often used decoratively in a wall. *Blank* or *blind arcading* means that the space inside the arches is filled with masonry, rather than a window or opening leading somewhere.

Arrow-slits. Narrow windows in a castle, etc., for archers to shoot from.

Ashlar. Building stones with their surface dressed to a smoothed finish.

Aumbry. A cupboard set into a wall; if in a church, for storing the Communion vessels.

Bailey. The open-air enclosed space between the keep of a castle and its curtain walls or palisades, often with domestic and working buildings in it. Associated with early Norman motte (mound) and bailey castles.

Baluster. In Anglo-Saxon architecture, a fairly short round shaft of equal circumference throughout its length, usually ornamented only by rings of varying widths.

Basilica. The characteristic plan of Roman early Christian and Byzantine Christian churches: a nave, with arcaded lower aisles and clerestory windows above the arcades, and a semi-circular apsed east end with altar.

Battlemented, crenellated, or embattled. Terms used to describe the top of a wall with regular rows of projecting rectangular 'teeth', common in castles. Hence, a decorative motif with regular rising and falling 'teeth', rectangular in outline (a common development from the usual zigzag of late Norman archways).

Beakhead. A favourite decorative motif around late Norman arches, etc., like a row of birds' or animals' (or even human) heads looking straight out from the stone and gripping a roll-moulding with their beaks or mouths.

Bell-opening. The aperture, like an unglazed window, in the wall of a tower at the level (bell stage) where the bells hang within.

Billet. A decorative motif like short sections of round rod with gaps between (often seen as billet and reel), frequently used in Norman carving from c. 1130 onwards.

Blank arcading. See *Arcading*.

Blind arcading. See *Arcading*.

Burh. Anglo-Saxon defended town (borough) surrounded by ditched banks and palisades.

Buttress. A vertical prop of stonework built against a wall, and projecting from it, for strength.

Cable. A decorative motif like a rope, fairly commonly found in late Norman carved ornament.

Capital. The stone, usually carved, on the top of a column or pier, and supporting the arch, etc., above (but see also *Abacus*). Anglo-Saxon capitals take varied forms, often primitive. *Cushion capitals* are typically early Norman, and the cuboid stones are carved in various ways, most frequently *scalloped* (like the curved ridges of a scallop shellfish) or *voluted* (with curling scrolls at the corners, descended from the Classical Ionic capital). *Sculpted capitals* (with human, etc., figures) were introduced to Anglo-Norman architecture in c. 1130–40, though a few may be earlier. *Bell capitals* (with a shape like their name, and often with waterleaf carving) were introduced to England by Cistercian monks in c. 1140–50.

Cashel. A walled or fenced and banked enclosure for a monastery of the Celtic Church, in the Irish and Scottish tradition.

Chancel. The eastern part of a church, containing the altar and for the use of priests only. Sometimes subdivided into sanctuary or presbytery with the altar, and choir where an organised chorus sings. The chancel was usually apsed at the east end in Anglo-Saxon and early Norman churches, and square-ended in later Norman times.

Chancel arch. The arch over the meeting point of chancel and (usually) nave.

Chapter house. The hall in a monastery, nunnery or canons' establishment in which the ecclesiastical and materialistic business of the brethren or sisters was discussed and decided.

Chevron. A motif like the letter V. See *Zigzag.*

Choir. The part of a church where the choir or chorus sings during services, often with seating called choir-stalls.

Clas (plural *clasau*). Welsh word, used especially for the colleges of learned and pious men and women of the pre-Norman Celtic Church living monastically, but as canons. Often associated with enclosed circular churchyards, some of which survive in part.

Clerestory. A windowed upper level of an enclosed space, especially of a nave, rising above the roof of the lower aisles on either side, and thus allowing daylight to enter.

Cloister. An open green rectangular space, usually in a monastery or nunnery, with roofed and arcaded walks around it, for the inmates' meditative exercising.

Corbel. A structural stone feature projecting from a wall, and often sculpted, to support the ribs of a roofing vault.

Corbel-table. A horizontal string-course, high in the outside wall of a church, punctuated by projecting carved stone heads.

Crenellation. See *Battlemented.*

Crossing. The space where the axis of the nave and chancel crosses that of the transepts in a cruciform church. Strictly speaking, a true crossing has nave, chancel and transepts all of the same height and width, but this hardly ever occurs in Anglo-Saxon churches.

Cruciform. Cross-shaped in plan.

Crypt. The underground room or rooms beneath the chancel or (occasionally) nave of a church. Originally built as places for pilgrims to view venerated relics.

Curtain wall. Wall, with sentry-walk along its top, around an open-air enclosure or bailey, usually punctuated with wall-towers.

Diaper. A decorative motif of plain checkers or diagonal squares of different materials or colours.

Dog-tooth. A decorative motif introduced in the very late Norman period (but commoner in the Early English Gothic that followed), with the points of earlier zigzag now developed into individual three-dimensional chevrons, each of four small shafts or leaves coming together in one projecting point.

Dormitory. Shared sleeping hall in a monastic institution.

Double-splay. See *Splay.*

Drum-pier. See *Pier.*

Extrados. The outer side of the curve of an arch (see the diagram of an arch on page 10).

Fish-scale. A decorative motif like the overlapping scales of a fish, fairly common in late Norman carved decoration.

Forebuilding. A subsidiary projecting building in front of a castle keep (or occasionally a church), containing the main entrance.

Fretwork. An ornamental motif in Celtic and some Anglo-Saxon carving, especially of stone crosses, consisting of diagonal patterning like multiple Greek key-pattern.

Gallery. In Romanesque architecture, the upper level arcade, above the ground-level arcades of the nave or chancel, etc., and below the windows of the clerestory. Later, in Gothic architecture, usually called the triforium.

Garderobe. Latrine emptying into water or just outside the castle or building (see also *Reredorter*).

Groin-vault. See *Vault.*

Hall. In Anglo-Saxon or Norman buildings, the main shared living room, for shelter, eating and sleeping.

Hall-keep. See *Keep.*

Herringbone. Stone walling with alternate rows of stone set diagonally one way and then diagonally the other, producing a multiple zigzag effect.

Hood-mould. A projecting outer band of an arch, basically to provide a part-roof preventing water from running on to the ornament of the arch, but later developing into a decorative feature itself.

Hospital. In Norman times, a building to provide hospitality for guests or travellers, or for the aged and infirm, as a charitable dwelling.

Impost. A stone band running along the wall horizontally from the level of the capital of an archway (see the diagram of an arch on page 10).

Incised pier. See *Pier.*

Interlace. Relief carving with intertwining trails of various kinds, typical of Celtic, Norse and some Anglo-Saxon ornament.

Jamb. The walling beside the vertical lower part of an archway (see the diagram of an arch on page 10).

Keep. The central defensive but habitable building of Norman castles. *Hall-keep*: a rectangular (later often round) keep with more than one storey, and several rooms including a living hall. *Shell-keep*: a keep with unroofed walls, often circular in plan, with sentry-walks around and space for domestic buildings within.

Lantern. A space inside a tower, with windows allowing daylight into the ground-level spaces below.

Lavatorium. A room for washing in a monastery.

Lesene (or *pilaster-strip*). An ornamental architectural feature much used in late Anglo-Saxon buildings. Narrow strips of stone embedded in the outer surface of a wall (of stone, often with a hard cement rendering) to form lines and patterns on its surface in the shape of oblongs, arches, triangles, etc.

Light (as in single-light or two-light window). An opening in a wall enclosed by stone, etc., surrounds and usually arched. The typical Norman domestic window is of two lights (each round-arched) under a higher arch enclosing both lights.

Long-and-short work. A common feature of late Anglo-Saxon architecture especially in corners (see *Quoin*) and the sides of doorways, with large long stones placed alternately vertically and horizontally above each other.

Lozenge-pattern. A decorative motif developed from the usual zigzag in late Norman carved ornament, with two or more lines of zigzag arranged so that their corners touch, thus forming a series of lozenges.

Mason. The craftsman who cuts and builds with stone, the master mason combining such skills with those of the building designer.

Masonry. Walling of shaped stones.

Medallion. A late Norman decorative motif, like a rosette, in rows around doorways, each medallion carved differently. Found in carving after 1180.

Megalithic. In Anglo-Saxon building, wall masonry formed of especially large stones. (The word megalith is derived from the Greek, and means simply Great Stone.)

Motte. A man-made mound of earth, usually with a wooden tower or keep on top of it, and a palisaded open-air enclosure or bailey on one side.

Moulding. The carved ornamental lines, grooves and rolls running around an arch, etc.

Narthex. A covered space at the west end of a church (especially Anglo-Saxon), but open to the air, often with an arcade, on its west (outer) side.

Nave. The main westerly part of a church, where the lay public attends services.

Order. In Anglo-Saxon and Norman architecture, a pair of shafts or columns and the arch bridging them; thus, a two-order doorway or other opening has two pairs of shafts and two-banded (moulded) arch, and so on up to the six-order doorways of, for example, Fountains Abbey, or even more.

Palisade. A defensive fence or wall of strong timber posts or tree trunks.

Parlatorium. A monastic room in which normally silent monks or nuns could talk to each other.

Pele-tower. A type of single-tower castle typical of the English borders with Scotland.

Pelta motif. A carved ornamental pattern like swirling interlaced ribbons, used on some Celtic and Anglo-Saxon stone crosses, etc.

Pier. The usual term for the pillars, columns or multiple-shafted supports of Romanesque (or Gothic) arches in arcades. *Drum-pier*: a thick round pier. *Composite pier*: a pier with many vertical shafts carved around its surface. *Incised pier*: a pier with large patterns (zigzags, spirals, checkers, etc.) carved deeply into its surface.

Pilaster-strip. See *Lesene.*

Porch. A sheltered space projecting as a small forebuilding in front of the entrance doorway to a building.

Portico. A multiple, and often ornately carved, projecting arched doorway to a building.

Porticus. A plural word meaning, literally, 'little porches'. In early Anglo-Saxon churches, they were low-arched side openings off the main space of the church, to the north or south, with a small chamber. If off the chancel, the Communion vessels, etc., were kept in the *porticus.* If off the nave or *narthex,* etc., offerings from the congregation were put there before presentation at the altar. Some *porticus* were also used for the tombs of holy people and for quietly meditative prayer. In late Anglo-Saxon churches (e.g. at Worth) the openings became larger and the *porticus* seem to have become incipient transepts.

Quadripartite. Of four parts or curving surfaces, especially of vaulting.

Quoin. Corner of a building where two walls meet, used especially in Anglo-Saxon architecture (see *Long-and-short work*).

Rebate. A groove in the inner side wall of an archway (see the diagram of an arch on page 10).

Reel. A decorative motif rather like a series of wide Hs or narrow-waisted cotton-reels (often combined in rows with billet-pattern), used in Norman carving from c. 1130 onwards.

Refectory. The hall in a monastery or nunnery where meals are served, often with a special pulpit from which readings of the gospels are given while the inmates eat.

Reredorter. Latrine, usually discharging into a river. A monastic term (see also *Garderobe*).

Respond. A half-shaft running up the vertical inner side wall of an archway (see the diagram of an arch on page 10).

Reveal. The vertical inner side wall of an archway (see the diagram of an arch on page 10).

Rhenish Helm. An early type of steeple capping a church tower, derived from Rhineland Romanesque churches, with the four flat sloping surfaces of the steeple set at diagonal angles to the four walls of the tower beneath (see illustration on page 41).

Rib-vault. See *Vault*.

Roll-moulding. A decorative feature around an arch, etc., roundly moulded like an elongated sausage.

Romanesque. The style shared by western European countries between the fall of the Roman Empire in the 500s and the development of the Gothic style around 1200. Derived from Classical Roman architecture, typical Romanesque features include solid masses of wall, rounded arches, flat or tunnel-vaulted roofs, often with massive piers to support arcades.

Rosette. In late Norman architecture, a decorative motif of flat circles with concentric or other carving within each.

Common from 1140s onwards and later developing into medallions.

Scallop. See *Capital*.

Shell-keep. See *Keep*.

Slype. The passage from the transept of a church into the cloister of a monastery, etc.

Soffit. The underside of an arch (see the diagram of an arch on page 10).

Solar. The proprietor's private chamber in a Norman castle or house, combining day use with bedroom.

Spandrel. The roughly triangular area of wall above the curve of an arch (see the diagram of an arch on page 10), or between two arches in an arcade, etc.

Splay. The wall at the sides of a window or other aperture cut away diagonally to admit or spread more daylight. *Double-splay:* with the walls cut away both inside and outside the window.

Stilted (as in stilted arch or apse). In elevation, a rounded arch raised on straight sides, from its capital and abacus, before it starts to curve. In plan, a rounded apse joined to the next space (e.g. the nave) by straight walls.

String-course. A narrow and slightly projecting horizontal band of stone around a building, a typical feature in late Anglo-Saxon and Norman buildings.

Tower arch. The arch over the opening from a tower into (usually) the nave of a church.

Tracery. Ribs of stone in various patterns supporting the glass of large windows (a post-Norman feature).

Transept. The spaces projecting north and south of a church, to form the side arms of a cross-shaped plan, and meeting the nave and chancel at the crossing.

Transitional. Term used to describe the buildings showing a transition between the solid-walled and round-arched Romanesque style and the more open-spaced and pointed-arched Gothic style, often combining features of both, c. 1180–1200.

Transverse moulding. Moulding on the under-surface (soffit) of an arch, e.g. zigzag projecting outwards from a wall, rather than lying flat on it.

Triangular-headed arch. A widespread late Anglo-Saxon feature, with two straight diagonal stones meeting at the top, rather than a curved arch.

Tunnel-vault. See *Vault*.

Tympanum. A semi-circular panel, usually sculpted, within the curve under a Romanesque arch and usually above a door.

Undercroft. The rib-vaulted (see *Vault*) ground-floor space, often open at the sides, under a hall or other first-floor room. A typical feature of Norman domestic and monastic architecture.

Vault. Stone, etc., roofing over a space. *Tunnel-vault*: roof formed like a flat-surfaced tunnel. *Groin-vault*: roof formed by angled quadripartite, etc., surfaced vaults, but without ribs where the surfaces meet. *Rib-vault*: roof formed by angled vaults, with stone ribs along (and supporting) the meeting lines of surfaces.

Volute. A curled scroll. See *Capital.*

Voussoir. The wedge-shaped stones that form the inner layer of an arch (see the diagram of an arch on page 10).

Ward. The open-air enclosure or courtyard of a castle, surrounded by walls and towers (see also *Bailey*).

Waterleaf. An ornamental carved motif of various sorts of leaves in the capitals of piers or corbels, introduced to England by Cistercian monks as their only carved ornament, c. 1140 and in widespread use in c. 1170–90.

Zigzag (or *chevron*) decoration. The chevron is a V, and this most widespread carved ornament on Norman arches, etc., first introduced in c. 1110, consists of a row of Vs touching each other. Sometimes there are many rows together, forming *multiple zigzag*, or the points of two rows touch each other, forming *lozenges* between the lines. Late in the Norman period, zigzag often projects from the wall, as well as lying along it.

BIBLIOGRAPHY

Brown, G. Baldwin, *The Arts in Early England*, especially Vols II, V and VI, London, 1910–30.

Clapham, Sir Alfred, *English Romanesque Architecture*, Vol. I, *Before the Conquest*; Vol. II, *After the Conquest*, Oxford, 1930 (reprinted 1969).

Conant, K. J., *Carolingian and Romanesque Architecture 800–1200*, Harmondsworth, 1959 (revised edition 1973).

Cruden, S. H., *The Early Christian and Pictish Monuments of Scotland*, London, HMSO, 1964.

Deanesly, Margaret, *A History of the Medieval Church 590–1500*, London, 1925 (revised edition 1969).

Forde-Johnston, J., *A Guide to the Castles of England and Wales*, London, 1981 (and other works by this author).

Palmer, R. Liddlesdale, *English*

Monasteries in the Middle Ages, London, 1930.

Renn, D. F., *Norman Castles in Britain*, London, 1973.

Stenton, Doris M., *English Society in the Early Middle Ages*, Harmondsworth, 1951 (revised edition 1965).

Talbot Rice, D., *English Art 871–1100*, Oxford, 1952.

Taylor, H. M. and Joan, *Anglo-Saxon Architecture*, Vols I, II and III, Cambridge, 1965–78.

Toy, S., *The Castles of Great Britain*, London, 1953.

Wood, Margaret, *The English Mediaeval House*, London, 1981.

Zarnecki, G., *English Romanesque Sculpture 1066–1140*, London, 1951. *Later English Romanesque Sculpture 1140–1210*, London, 1953.

ILLUSTRATION ACKNOWLEDGEMENTS

Plans are reproduced on the pages specified, by permission, from the following sources:

Sir Alfred Clapham, *English Romanesque Architecture*, Oxford University Press, 1969 (16, 25, 64, 113, 115); D. M. Wilson, *The Archaeology of Anglo-Saxon England*, Methuen (29); *DoE Illustrated Guides*, Crown Copyright by permission of the Controller of Her Majesty's Stationery

Office (52); *Abbeys, Illustrated Guide*, Crown Copyright by permission of the Controller of Her Majesty's Stationery Office, 1976 (104); Margaret Wood, *The English Mediaeval House*, Ferndale Editions, 1981 (85).